YOUR DOG & PUPPY

Your Dog & Puppy

Published by:
Greatest Guides Limited, Woodstock, Bridge End, Warwick
CV34 6PD, United Kingdom

www.greatestguides.com

Greatest Guides is committed to a sustai[n]
planet. This book is printed on paper cer[t]
Stewardship Council.

MIX
Paper
FSC   FSC® C020837

Printed and bound in the United Kingdo[m]

ISBN 978-1-907906-07-7

To my wonderful wife Jenny
for all her love and support

Contents

Introduction...

Writing Your Dog & Puppy sounded like a pretty
straightforward assignment – after all, I've been a vet for
over fifteen years, and before that I spent five years learning
everything there is to know about the inner workings of dogs
at Bristol vet school. However, when I sat down in front of my
computer and pondered the task in front of me, every idea I
had for a useful tip seemed to come from elsewhere – I was
never taught at vet school that garlic keeps fleas away, or that
feeding cotton wool can save a dog's life. Instead, I found
myself drawing on all the experiences I've had with dogs
since I qualified, from dealing with patients at the surgery to
bringing up my lovely two collie crosses at home.

From carrying Pan and Badger home from the farm in Devon
where they came from, to losing them repeatedly on Cleeve
Hill in Cheltenham, my experiences as a 'father' to these
wonderful dogs has had far more influence on the content
you're about to read than my veterinary training ever did. Of
course, there is plenty of good vet science in these pages, but
I hope I've also managed to convey the truly personal nature
of dog ownership. This book is not meant as a comprehensive
encyclopaedia of dog knowledge – think of it more as a
guidebook to help you negotiate the sometimes tricky path of
dog ownership.

Dip into it as you feel the urge or the need, and take on board the advice that applies to you and your dog – but above all, never forget that you and your dog are a special team and there's very little that good old common sense and TLC won't sort out!

Good luck!

Joe Inglis

Choosing a New Dog

" I think dogs are the most amazing creatures; they give unconditional love. For me they are the role model for being alive. "

Gilda Radner

Chapter 1
Choosing a New Dog

Bringing a new dog into your life and home requires plenty of planning and dedication, be it a little puppy or a full-grown adult. Getting it wrong can be a disaster for you and for your new best friend, so here are a few key points to make sure you make the right decisions:

ARE YOU READY FOR A DOG?

So you're thinking about getting a dog? Perhaps it will be your first ever pet or maybe the new arrival will need to fit into a busy family of animals. Whatever your situation, you need to do some serious thinking before committing yourself – and your new dog – to a life together. Don't forget the truth behind the old saying 'a dog is for life, not just for Christmas'. Dogs can live for twenty years or more, so make sure you're ready to share your life for the foreseeable future!

IS YOUR HOUSE READY FOR A DOG?

Owning a dog is more than just walks in the park and dog bowls in the kitchen. If you take a dog into your life, you need to make sure your house is a suitable home for your new canine companion – and also consider how sharing your home with a dog will change things for you and your family.

Are you ready to say goodbye to spotless sofas and clean carpets and say hello to muddy paw-prints and furry furniture? Are you ready to give up a perfectly manicured flowerbed in exchange for a well-dug doggy garden?

If you're not sure, why not pay a visit to some friends who have a dog? If you find yourself perched uncomfortably on the sofa, picking dog hairs off your trousers, maybe a dog isn't for you. But if the sight of Fido demolishing your friend's daffodils or peeing in their wisteria relaxes you, it's time to start thinking about which dog will suit you best!

PUPPY OR ADULT?

When most people take on a new dog, it's usually a puppy. Sharing those early weeks and months, when the puppy is a bundle of cute, cuddly fun, is a wonderful experience, and interacting with an animal at this age is the best way to make a really strong, life-long bond.

However, getting a puppy is not your only option. Many people prefer to take on an older dog, either from a friend or a rescue center. Maybe you don't want the hassle of training a boisterous new puppy, or perhaps you're elderly and don't feel it's fair to take on a young dog. But whatever your circumstances, it's well worth considering an adult dog, especially when you consider how many languish, unloved in rescue centers. Giving one of these abandoned dogs a new home and a new life can be just as rewarding as taking on a puppy.

CHOOSING THE RIGHT BREED

How do you go about choosing the right dog for you? After all, there are hundreds of different breeds, from giants like Afghan hounds to tiny terriers like the Jack Russell, not to mention the infinite variety of cross breeds that come in almost every shape, size and temperament.

To choose the best dog for you, the best approach it to start by narrowing your choices down. Do you want a big dog or a little one, a manic mutt or a passive pet, a long-haired dog or a short-haired one? And think about why you are getting a dog. If you would like to show or breed, then think about a pedigree dog, if not, a cross-breed might suit you best. And then, do your research. Read up about the breeds you're interested in to find out about their character, their potential pitfalls, and decide which one best suits your lifestyle.

If you don't live in a big house, or have a big garden, why not think about getting a terrier. They can be great companions and have wonderful personalities. My favorites are Jack Russells, which are very tough and loyal, and don't need as much exercise as many big dogs.

At the other end of the scale, lots of people love big dogs, whether as a status symbol, or for reassurance on night-time walks. There are lots of big breeds out there, from Wolfhounds to Mastiffs, but only consider taking one on if you've got the room and energy they require. Bigger dogs generally need more exercise and attention, and won't be happy cooped up in a tiny flat or house all day. They also tend to have shorter life spans than smaller dogs – in some cases, the average life-expectancy can be as short as 7 or 8 years.

And the final thing to remember is the bigger the dog, the bigger the bills. Everything, from food to vet bills, will be more expensive for a large dog, so make sure you can afford the dog of your dreams before you take him on.

Finally, the best way to really find out which breed is for you is to get out there and meet them – visit friends or breeders who own them, or spend an afternoon at the local rescue kennels. And don't forget dog shows, where you can chat to hundreds of breeders and enthusiasts and really find out whether it's a Poodle or a Papillion, a mongrel or a Manchester Terrier that's the one for you.

" There is no psychiatrist in the world like a puppy licking your face. "

Bern Williams

JOE'S TOP FIVE BREEDS

Here are my personal favorites in the doggy world:

1. Border Collie – the most intelligent dog around, these lithe, energetic dogs, originally from the Scottish borders, can be a real handful, but no other breed can match them for brains and instincts. Only for those with plenty of time, energy and space!

2. Labrador – the opposite of the collie in terms of temperament – quiet, dependable and sensitive – Labradors are the ultimate family companions.

3. Jack Russell terrier – bred by the Reverend Jack Russell in the 19th century as a pocket-sized fox hound, the Jack Russell makes up in character what he lacks in size!

4. Beagle – one of the happiest breeds around, combining good looks with a friendly temperament and unusual longevity. Watch out for his voice though, as he can get a bit noisy if left alone.

5. Mongrel! – I know it's not a breed, but some of the finest dogs around have lots of mixed blood. It gives them plenty of so-called 'hybrid vigor' and they are much less prone to inherited diseases than many purebred dogs.

DID YOU KNOW?

Pharaoh Hounds are the only dogs that blush. They do this when they are excited or happy; their ears, nose and eyes become pink.

FINDING YOUR PERFECT DOG

Once you've decided on a breed or type of dog, now it's time to find him or her. But how exactly do you search out your perfect pooch?

There are many different places to look. If you're thinking about an older dog, or taking on a rescued puppy, then you should head straight down to your local animal rescue center. If a pedigree puppy is going to be your perfect partner then try your national Kennel Club association, which will be able to give you names and numbers for local breeders. And you could also visit your vet, who will know of any new litters on the way, and any dogs needing new homes.

Try and avoid pet shops and puppy farms, as the puppies they rear and sell are often unhealthy and poorly treated.

Never, ever buy a puppy without seeing where it was brought up and without meeting its mother (and father if possible). Some unscrupulous breeders and puppy farmers will try to get you to meet them somewhere, such as a service station, to hand over the puppy. Always say no to this – if they won't let you see their breeding establishment, it's usually because it's not up to standard and the puppy has been reared in terrible conditions.

When it comes to selecting a puppy from a litter, there are a few key things to look for when you're making your choice. Firstly, avoid puppies that are much smaller than the others. Very small puppies often don't thrive as well as their bigger brothers and sisters, and might be more prone to health problems later in life.

Then think about the character of the pup you want. If you want a bold, dominant dog, pick out the big fat pup that comes charging straight over to you. And if you would prefer a more laid back dog, look for the relaxed pup in the middle of the crowd. But, most of all, let your heart rule your head, and pick the pup you fall in love with. At the end of the day, bonding with your new dog is far more important than how he looks!

Before you pick up your new pup and rush her home, make sure she's the right age. Bitches will usually wean their puppies at between 5 and 7 weeks of age, and it's vital not to take puppies before this. If you take them too young, they might miss out on the vital antibodies and nutrients they get from their mother's milk.

On the other hand, leave them with their mother too long and you risk other kinds of problems. Dogs are most receptive to socialization and bonding between 8 weeks and 16 weeks, so it's vital your new dog is getting used to you and your home in this period. The best time to take a puppy is between 7 and 10 weeks, thereby ensuring that they get all the protection their mother's milk can offer, whilst being young enough to make that all-important bond with you and your family.

When your new family member comes home, it's important that they feel safe and comfortable in their new surroundings. Make sure there's a new, clean, dog bed waiting for him, as well as a full water bowl and a few toys to play with. If you've got other pets, it's worth keeping them out of the way for an hour or two while the new arrival finds his feet. Put the cat out or take the dog for a walk – and if the kids are going to be over-excited, maybe take them out for a walk, too!

The First Month

" Happiness is a warm puppy. "

Charles M Schulz

Chapter 2
The First Month

Making the right decisions about taking on a new dog is just the start. Now you've got your puppy home, the real hard work begins...

OPENING NIGHT!

With your new pup safely asleep on her bed, a nice meal of puppy food inside her and a contented look on her face, you sneak out of the kitchen and off to your own bed. You close your eyes and drift off, dreaming of happy puppies and country walks.

But then you are suddenly woken by a horrible, piercing cry of anguish, which seems to fill the whole house. You jump out of bed and rush to see what calamity could have befallen your precious puppy.

It's nothing serious, just a case of first night nerves, so you decide to let her have just this one night in your bed. She curls up happily next to you and everyone sleeps happily.

Wrong!

If you take this approach, prepare yourself to either share your bed with your dog for the rest of its life, or to put up with a howling puppy for many months to come.

The only solution is to be firm from day one, and teach your puppy that howling brings no reward. Endure one long night of howling without returning to comfort your puppy and she will never try it again. If you give in at 3am, she'll be sure to try the same tactic the next night – only this time she knows she might have to persist until at least the same time again.

It might sound harsh, but dog training is all about being firm and fair. Lay down your ground rules from day one, and you'll have a happy, well-behaved dog – and neighbors who still talk to you!

FEEDING YOUR PUPPY

When you have a new puppy, you take over from his mother and take on the responsibility for making sure he eats the right amount of the right food. Get this wrong, and it could affect your dog for the rest of his life.

The most important thing about feeding puppies is to offer them lots of meals. With their mother, they will have been feeding every three or four hours, so you need to feed a puppy at least four times a day when they are seven or eight weeks old. As time goes by, you can gradually reduce the number of feeds, down to two by the time they are about three months old.

There are many different dogs foods out there, but whichever one you choose, make sure it's suitable for puppies, as they have special nutritional requirements. It's best to offer a mixture of canned and dried foods, and feed the amount stated on the packaging – too much food at this age could lead to an overweight adult, and even cause serious health problems, like arthritis.

If you are keen on supplementing your puppy's diet with some home cooked food, here are some healthy recipes that you can feed them, alongside a complete puppy diet:

MEATY RICE PUDDING

Something of a treat, this recipe is packed full of wholesome nutrients – carbohydrate from the rice, protein from the meat and calcium from the milk. It takes a while to cook, and the recipe makes enough for several meals – but you can keep it in the fridge for a few days – or, better still, invite around a few friends with puppies and have a puppy party!

To make enough for a puppy party, you will require:

- 125g rice

- 750ml milk

- 150g beef or lamb mince

- 1 teaspoon yeast extract

Simply mix all the ingredients together in a large ovenproof dish. Pop it in a moderate oven (180C, Gas mark 4) for about 75 minutes. Stir frequently for the first 45 minutes and then leave alone for the final 30 minutes. Leave it to cool for at least an hour before serving.

PUPPY CHEESY TREATS

These tasty biscuits are an ideal treat or snack for a hungry puppy. Use them to help with training by rewarding good behavior – but make sure you don't overdo them as they are quite rich and fatty. One or two treats a day, as part of your training schedule, is ideal.

For enough treats to last a couple of weeks, you want:

- 250g whole-wheat flour

- 150g grated cheddar cheese

- 50g butter

- 1 clove garlic

- 1 beef stock cube

- Milk

Mix the flour and butter together in a large bowl and run the fat in until it forms a crumbly mixture. Then add in the grated cheese, crushed garlic and crumbled stock cube and mix well.

Slowly add milk to the mixture until it forms a very sticky dough. Flour your hands and start kneading the dough until it forms a single firm lump. Turn it out onto a floured surface and roll it out to about a ½ inch thick. Cut the dough up into puppy-sized biscuits using a small pastry cutter – or if you don't have one, try using the end of an apple corer – this cuts the dough into just the right sized little rounds.

Then place the biscuits onto a greased baking tray and cook in a moderate oven (180C, Gas Mark 4) for 15–20 minutes, until they are golden brown. Allow to cool and then store in an airtight container.

LIVER AND BANANA MILK SHAKE

Now this might sound pretty unpleasant to you, but puppies will go mad for this shake. It's full of the goodness of liver, and the fresh vitamins you can only get from fruit like bananas.

Either serve on its own or pour over his dried dog food – either way, he'll lap it up.

For enough for 2 or 3 puppy drinks, you'll need:

- Small piece of liver (about 100g)

- 1 banana

- ½ pint milk

Place the liver in a large bowl and cover it with boiling water. Leave it to cook for ten minutes and then drop it into a blender with the peeled banana and milk. Blend everything together (remember to put the lid on the blender – a mistake I've made once…) and serve straight away.

TOILET TRAINING

It's the first morning with your new puppy, and you walk into the kitchen to find a pile of pooh, a puddle of wee, and an apologetic-looking pup.

Should you a) shout at the puppy and rub their nose in the mess? b) Ignore the problem and clean everything up? Or c) let your puppy straight out into the garden or yard and praise them when they do their business outside?

The answer is, of course, c). Toilet training is all about positive reinforcement and encouragement, rather than punishment. Dogs, like all animals, are naturally clean, and nearly all dogs will get the hang of toilet training very quickly, given the right help and encouragement. Simply take your puppy into the garden at regular intervals, and praise him whenever he goes to the toilet outside.

Lots of people still use newspaper as a way of house training puppies, but, while it can help soak up some of the mess, it can delay the training process because it encourages the puppy to think it's okay to wee in the house – and on your papers. It's much better to whisk the puppy out into the garden at the first hint that he is about to go for a wee, and reward him with a titbit when he's just finished doing his business outside. It's also a good idea to take him out straight after he's eaten because this is when he's likely to want to go to the toilet.

If (well, when) your puppy has an accident in the house, it's important to clean it up straight away with a good cleaner specially designed to take the smell away. Most normal household cleaners won't get rid of the smell entirely, and any odor that lingers will encourage the puppy to wee in that spot again. Use a special anti-odor cleaner from your pet shop or vet because this will get rid of the smell completely every time.

PLAY TIME AND TOYS

A young puppy should be full of energy and enthusiasm for life, and needs plenty of entertainment to keep her fit and happy. Make sure you've got a few robust toys for her to play with, as games are a vital part of learning behavioral skills for a puppy, and spend as much time with her as you can. This will build up that bond between you and will also make sure she doesn't get bored – bored puppies turn into badly behaved dogs.

Play is also important for establishing the social order of the family, as, in the wild, dogs will use play to build relationships between the members of the pack, as well as being great physical training for hunting and scavenging. It's not about exerting dominance over your puppy, more about reinforcing the fact that you are both cooperating companions in the same social group.

Just a quick reminder not to be too rough with your new puppy, especially when playing tug of war. At this young age, their jaws will be weak and can be damaged if you play too violently with them.

Instead of wrenching the toy out of his mouth, teach him to drop it on command by offering a nice treat. As well as keeping his jaw in one piece, teaching him to drop is a really useful command – and one you could be very thankful for in later years when he's busy chewing your best slippers!

FIRST TRIP TO THE VETS

Within the first week of having your new puppy, it's well worth a trip to your local veterinary clinic to have a check up and find out about vaccinations, worming and all the other important topics you need know about. Most vets will offer this introductory check up free of charge.

If you've not been to a vet before, ask friends with dogs for their recommendation, and go see a few practices before settling on the one you feel most comfortable with. It's important to establish a good relationship with your vet, so choose one where you and your new puppy are made to feel welcome.

MY TOP TIPS FOR CHOOSING A GOOD VET

1. Small practices tend to be friendlier and it's easier to always see the same vet.

2. Out of hours in house – lots of vets have a dedicated out of hours service but this will cost you a lot of money if you have to use it, and you won't be dealing with your own vet.

3. Big flash new premises are all very well but don't forget that your fees are paying for it, and many of these big super practices have to charge a lot more than smaller practices as a result.

4. Parking is vital. This might sound like a minor point, but, when you've got a sick dog, the last thing you want is to spend hours looking for a parking place.

5. Make an appointment to meet the veterinarian as well as the staff. How do they interact with customers, as well as each other? While you're there, ask for a tour of the facility. It would be a good idea to not ask for the tour in advance. This way you can see how the facility is kept without being warned of a visitor.

6. Look for cleanliness, especially in the kennel area. If you see unclean kennels or droppings on the floor, it might mean they do not have enough staff to care for the animals. Hygiene is important because of the spread of diseases among animals.

7. Ask about emergency care? Is it even offered? Accidents can happen to your pet at anytime. Is there 24/7 emergency pet care? Find out whether, if your dog does have to stay overnight, there will be a member of staff staying with him.

8. Trust your dog! A good vet should treat your dog with care and affection and your dog is the best person to let you know how good your vet is in this area.

One of the most vital parts in looking after a new puppy is to have him vaccinated. This protects him against some really nasty diseases, including rabies, distemper, parvovirus and leptospirosis. Not long ago, before most dogs were routinely vaccinated, these diseases killed thousands of animals every year, so they really are an essential part of looking after your new friend.

The injections themselves are very small, and generally painless. Most vets will put the needle into the scruff, and this part of the skin is not at all sensitive to pain as it is where bitches pick up their puppies using their teeth.

The first injection should be given when your puppy is about eight weeks old, and the second two to four weeks later. Full protection comes a week after the second jab, so it's worth keeping away from parks and other communal spaces until then.

As well as inoculating your puppy, your veterinarian will be able to advise you about other aspects of your puppy's health, including worms and fleas.

WORMS

The idea of worms living inside your puppy's stomach is not very pleasant to think about, but, unfortunately, intestinal worms such as tapeworms and roundworms are very common, particularly in puppies. Worms can cause health problems for puppies and adult dogs, including weight loss, poor condition and skin problems, but, more seriously, one species of worm can also pose a very real health risk to people and children in particular.

The roundworm toxocara canis, which is most commonly found in puppies, can cause serious health complications in children, including blindness if the larvae of the worms damage the eyes, which can happen in rare cases. Therefore, treating worms is not just essential for the wellbeing of your puppy, it's also crucial for the health and safety of our children.

Thankfully, preventing and treating worms has never been easier thanks to modern worming preparations, and there is no excuse for all pet owners not to be keeping their pets – and their families – safe from worms.

1. Worm puppies and kittens every 2 weeks – this is the period when roundworms are most prevalent and they are passed across the placenta and in the milk from the mother so it is crucial to worm regularly at this time.

2. Worm adult dogs and cats at least every 3 months – this is the generally accepted minimum interval for dogs and cats, but you should worm monthly if your cats are regular hunters, as this is one of the main sources of worms, or if your dogs live very active outdoor lifestyles.

3. Use good quality wormers – just like with fleas, you get what you pay for and cheap wormers from pet shops are likely to be ineffective.

FLEAS

Fleas are probably the best known parasites of cats and dogs and are incredibly common, with most pets suffering from a flea infestation at least once in their lives. Although there are over 2000 species of flea in the world, only 2 commonly affect dogs and cats – so called dog and cat fleas. Fleas live on blood sucked through the skin of their hosts using sharp, probing mouth parts, and while the amount of blood lost is usually insignificant except in very young or infirm animals, fleas can cause a range of health problems for their hosts.

The most obvious and common problem is skin disease and this is often caused by an allergic reaction to the flea's saliva (which is considered one of the most allergenic substances on earth!), which makes their host itchy – and itching then leads to skin damage, hair loss and secondary infections. In the worst cases, animals can be left practically bald and covered in sores if flea infestations are left unchecked.

As well as causing skin problems, fleas can also transmit other parasites, specifically one of the most common species of tapeworm, which is passed onto the host when they eat the fleas that contain the larvae of the tapeworm.

Controlling and preventing fleas is an important part of looking after your puppy and there are many ways to do this, including sprays, drops and tablets.

1. Check your puppy regularly for fleas – look in the fur at the base of their tail for the tell-tale black specs (flea dirt) and the fleas themselves (tiny brown insects that move very fast!).

2. Prevention is better than cure – so use a flea control product regularly to prevent infestations.

3. Don't let your guard down in the winter – in modern centrally heated houses, fleas can breed and flourish in the winter as well as summer, so you need to protect your pet all year round.

4. Treat the house as well as the dog – if you do have a flea problem, you need to treat the house with an insecticidal spray as well as your pet as up to 90% of the problem can be in the carpets and bedding, which is where the larvae and eggs will be.

5. You get what you pay for – avoid cheap and cheerful flea preparations from pet shops and supermarkets as they won't work. It's better (and cheaper in the long run) to use proper products from your vet.

If you're not sure if your lovely new puppy has got fleas, here's a tip to help you find out:

Take a sheet of white paper, and then use a fine comb to go through your puppy's fur, especially along his back. Comb onto the piece of paper, and collect whatever comes out of the coat. If you find lots of tiny black specks, this could be flea dirt. To check, dab the specks with a piece of wet cotton wool. If it is flea dirt, the cotton wool will get stained red thanks to the blood in the dirt.

MICROCHIPS

Thousands of dogs are lost and stolen every year, and getting them back can be almost impossible, because it's often your word against the new 'owner's'. However, my next tip is a really effective way of making sure your new puppy is always identified as your dog.

TEN THINGS YOU MIGHT NOT KNOW ABOUT YOUR PUPPY…

1. A puppy is born blind, deaf and toothless.

2. During its first week, 90% of a puppy's time is spent sleeping and 10% eating.

3. A puppy is only able to crawl during its first week.

4. A puppy begins to see when it is between 2 to 3 weeks old.

5. During the ages of 3 to 7 weeks, a puppy's first teeth, or milk teeth will appear.

6. At the age of 3 weeks, a puppy will develop its sense of smell.

7. A puppy will sleep for 14 hours every day.

8. A puppy's adult teeth start to come through between 4 and 8 months when it starts to chew everything!

9. A puppy is considered an adult at the age of one year. At this age, it is as physically mature as a 15 year-old human.

10. Bulldog puppies are delivered by caesarean section because of their large heads.

What you need to do is have a tiny microchip implanted in his neck. This contains a unique number, which is held along with your details, on a national database.

Your vet can implant the chip using a needle (really don't look at this one – it's pretty big!) and once it's in place, it's there for life, and can be easily read using a special scanner.

And if you want the ultimate in dog protection, you could consider using the latest identification technology – DNA swabbing. A swab is taken from your dog's mouth and this can be used to prove the identity of your dog beyond doubt in a court of law.

Adolescence

" I used to look at my dog Smokey and think, 'If you were a little smarter you could tell me what you were thinking', and he'd look at me like he was saying, 'If you were a little smarter, I wouldn't have to.' **"**

Fred Jungclaus

Chapter 3
Adolescence

So, the first month has passed, and everything is going well. Worms, fleas and injections are all sorted, so surely it's plain sailing from here on? Sorry to disappoint, but the next few months are just as crucial as the first, because your puppy is starting to grow up – and we all know that can spell trouble!

For many people, when they think about taking on a new dog, their big fear is that it won't get on with the kids – and maybe it'll even bite them. While this can be a worry, especially if you have a bigger breed dog, here are a few key things to remember, which should prevent any problems.

Firstly, it's important to remember that dogs in the wild live in well-ordered social groups, with clearly defined relationships between members of the group. While the pack theory of behavior, with its focus on dominance as the primary factor in dog relationships, is seen as much less valid nowadays thanks to advances in the study of wild dogs, it is still important to establish clear social relationships so your dog knows their place in the family.

To do this, lay down some clear house rules from day one that make it clear where the boundaries lie for your dog. For example, keep the dog downstairs and off the sofa, and make sure he doesn't get his dinner until after you and children have had yours. If you stick to this approach, you should never have problems with an over-dominant dog in the family.

The second tip to stop your dog from causing trouble with the kids is to put all of her toys in a box the kids control. When they want to play with her, they get the box out and give the dog a toy to play with. At the end of the game, the kids pick up the toys and put them back in the box. This way, the dog knows that the toys are controlled by the children and this will help reinforce the social order in the family.

And my final tip for dealing with a teenage dog that's getting above his station is to use a bit of door discipline. What this means is that everyone in the family, from the baby to granny, should always go through doors before the dog. Make him wait, especially when you're going out of the front or back door. He should sit obediently until you've opened the door, walked through, and called him.

SOCIALIZATION

The world can be a confusing place for a young dog, and so it's not surprising that they can get very upset by some of the stranger things we expect them to cope with.

Take cars for example. They may seem very normal and mundane to us, but to a dog that has never seen the world move in front of his eyes like that, they can be very scary indeed! And a scared dog, barking and growling at the steering wheel, is no fun for anyone.

The best tip for avoiding these kinds of problems is to introduce your dog to anything likely to cause fear at an early stage so he can get used to it while his mind is still open to new ideas. This window of opportunity generally lasts until they are about four months old – so as soon as your dog is fully protected with his vaccinations, get him out and about meeting and greeting!

Things to get your dog used to…

- Going in the car

- Meeting people in wheelchairs

- People on bicycles

- Kids on skateboards

- Shopping trolleys

- Cats

- Farm animals

And last but not least, don't forget... men with beards! (A surprising number of unsocialized dogs will bark and growl at a bearded man and it can get a little embarrassing!)

AGGRESSION

There's nothing worse than a dog that launches into a mad frenzy of barking and biting whenever he sees another dog. It ruins those quiet country strolls, not to mention the potential for a really nasty bite for any poor dog who gets attacked (or any person who gets caught in the crossfire).

So how do you prevent your dog from being aggressive to other dogs? Well, the best approach is get your puppy used to other dogs at an early stage. Much like socializing him with cars and bicycles, you've got to get him used to interacting with other dogs when he's young enough to learn the lesson. And the best way to do this is to go to a puppy party.

Now you might be wondering what on earth a puppy party is – if you were expecting music and dancing dachshunds then you're in for a disappointment! Puppy parties are, in fact, all about new puppies meeting each other and getting the hang of all those vital social skills that are key to avoiding trouble when they're older. They usually take place at vets or puppy training schools, and any puppies that have had their first vaccinations are welcomed along.

As well as meeting lots of other puppies, these parties are also an opportunity for new 'parents' to learn more about training and general health issues.

JOINING THE FAMILY

If you've got an older dog in the family and you bring along a new pup, the old dog can have his nose put out of joint by all the attention and fuss the new puppy is getting. Make sure you don't forget to give the old boy lots of walks and cuddles, as this will reassure him that the new whippersnapper hasn't taken over the family entirely.

Another thing to watch out for, if you already have a dog when you bring along a puppy, is trouble between the two of them. In time, the puppy might well become the dominant dog in the family, but until she is old enough and confident enough to take on the older dog's crown, you should make sure you reinforce the older dog's position as top dog. Feed him first and give him pats and cuddles before you give attention to the puppy. This way she will know her place and be less likely to cause trouble, and the old boy will be reassured and not feel the need to be aggressive to the pup.

PUPPIES AND BABIES

If you're brave enough to have taken on a new puppy at the same time as having a baby, then there are a few extra things to remember. Firstly, never leave the dog and baby alone together – you can never predict a dog's behavior 100% and it's not worth taking any risks. Secondly, make sure that the dog gets used to the baby as soon as possible (under supervision of course) – and also gets used to the fact that the baby is well above him in the pack order. And finally, take extra care with hygiene as dogs can pose a health risk to babies and young children via roundworm eggs and bacteria in their feces.

PUPPY CRATES

Giving pup a place of her own in the form of a puppy crate is a modern idea that can work really well for juvenile dogs. The crates are basically large cages, and they work by giving the pup somewhere of her own to spend time, and helps to train and discipline her. If you want to use a crate,

" The greatest pleasure of a dog is that you may make a fool of yourself with him, and not only will he not scold you, but he will make a fool of himself, too. "

Samuel Butler

make sure you buy a big enough one for your dog, and line it with a comfy bed. Encourage her to spend time in there every day, but leave the door open as much as you can. It's also a good idea to feed her in the crate and occasionally put a treat in there so she associates being in there with good things.

The crate shouldn't be used as a 'sin-bin' for hours on end, but they can be very useful for keeping an un-supervised puppy out of mischief, or as somewhere for an over-excited puppy to go to calm down for a while – much like sending a troublesome teenager to their room!

And, of course, there's just one more thing to remember – she's got to look good, so pick a lead and collar that suits her coloring and breed!

Before you get too carried away, remember that you should never take your dog out in public areas or parks until a week after their second puppy vaccination. Diseases like distemper and parvovirus are still around, and unvaccinated dogs can pick them up from other dogs, and even foxes.

When you first start taking your dog out in parks and woods, try to avoid the busy times when there are loads of dogs and people about. This will help your dog get used to all the interesting smells and sights of the countryside, without the added excitement of lots of other dogs.

To begin with, always keep your puppy on the lead. An overexcited puppy can easily disappear into the undergrowth and not be seen for hours, so it's best to keep him under control until he's got used to the park and you've done some basic training.

Having a familiar daily routine is really important for young dogs, so try to get into the habit of walking her at roughly the same time every day. A good walk first thing and then again in the early evening is the minimum any dog should get – but, ideally, take her out for three walks if you have the time.

One of the biggest mistakes people make with young dogs is over-exercising them. Overdoing energetic walks – especially when the dog is doing lots of running – can cause serious health problems later in life. The main problem is joint disease (arthritis), and this is particularly serious in larger dogs. If they do too much running and jumping when their joints are still developing (up to two years of age for really big dogs), the cartilage can be damaged and this can leave them with permanent problems, including severe lameness.

Some experts recommend that big dogs should have no off-lead exercise at all until they are two years old, but most vets advise a slightly less strict regime. The key tip is to take your dog for lots of short walks, mainly on the lead, rather than going out for long periods in one go.

OUT AND ABOUT

One of the best things about owning a dog is the exercise you both get. Two walks a day, come rain or shine, does wonders for both you and your new friend, but there are a few things to be aware of before you go racing off across the hills.

Firstly, it's crucial to equip him with a suitable lead and collar. Being able to safely and effectively restrain your dog is essential, especially when you're walking him on roads.

There are hundreds of different styles and sizes to choose from but here are a few key things to remember:

- A collar will be on your dog all the time, so make sure it is well-made and comfortable.

- Never use choke chains as these can be very dangerous and painful.

- Dogs with thin and delicate necks, such as greyhounds, lurchers and whippets, should have extra wide collars so they don't dig in and cause damage.

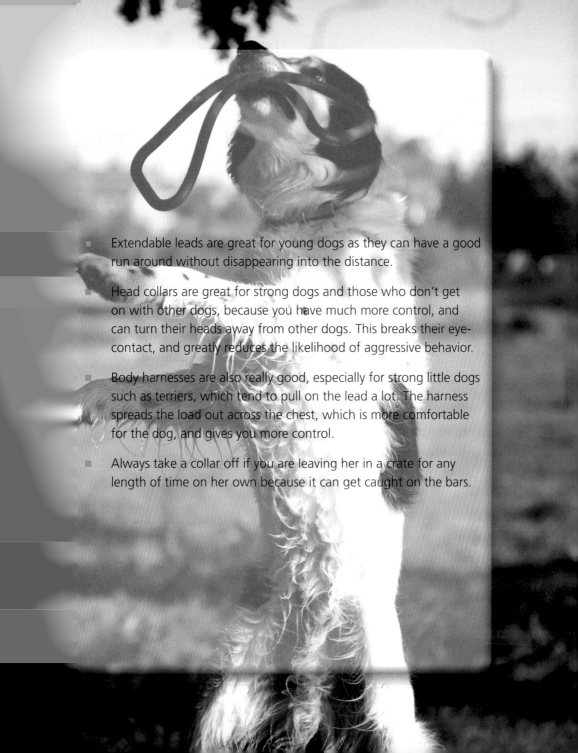

- Extendable leads are great for young dogs as they can have a good run around without disappearing into the distance.

- Head collars are great for strong dogs and those who don't get on with other dogs, because you have much more control, and can turn their heads away from other dogs. This breaks their eye-contact, and greatly reduces the likelihood of aggressive behavior.

- Body harnesses are also really good, especially for strong little dogs such as terriers, which tend to pull on the lead a lot. The harness spreads the load out across the chest, which is more comfortable for the dog, and gives you more control.

- Always take a collar off if you are leaving her in a crate for any length of time on her own because it can get caught on the bars.

DID YOU KNOW?

Most dogs, it seems, are born to run. They can run for long periods of time and over long distances. What makes them so well adapted for running? Lots of things!

As a dog runs, its body works like a bellows. A galloping dog takes one breath with each stride. When its back extends, it's easy for the lungs to expand and the dog inhales. When its back flexes, the lungs are compressed, squeezing out air, and the dog exhales.

The long, lean legs of many dogs make running a breeze because it takes relatively little energy to pump them back and forth. Dogs with the longest legs relative to their body size are usually the fastest runners because they take the longest strides. Dogs with shorter, squat legs are usually not very fast runners.

Hard-working muscles need lots of oxygen. Without that extra oxygen, muscles tire and begin to ache, causing both dogs and us to slow down. When dogs run, their heart rate skyrockets, pumping oxygen-rich blood to the muscles. In fact, a snoozing dog has a heart rate about the same as a resting human, 80 beats per minute. A working dog's heart rate can reach 274 beats a minute, almost double the rate of a healthy, active human. No wonder dogs can keep going after most people are exhausted!

Red blood cells, made in the spleen, carry oxygen throughout the body. An exercising dog dumps extra red blood cells into its bloodstream, increasing the amount of oxygen in its blood. This helps prevent muscle fatigue.

DID YOU KNOW?

Of all a dog's senses, its sense of smell is the most highly developed.

Dogs have about 25 times more olfactory (smell) receptors than humans do. These receptors occur in special sniffing cells deep in a dog's snout and are what allow a dog to "out-smell" humans.

Dogs can sense odors at concentrations nearly 100 million times lower than humans can. They can detect one drop of blood in five 1½ gallons of water! Sniffing the bare pavement may seem crazy, but it yields a wealth of information to your dog, whether it's the scent of the poodle next door or a whiff of the bacon sandwich someone dropped last week.

When a dog breathes normally, air doesn't pass directly over the smell receptors. But when the dog takes a deep sniff, the air travels all the way to the smell receptors, near the back of the dog's snout. So, for a dog, sniffing is a big part of smelling.

A dog can sniff out all sorts of smells that human noses miss. Because of this keen sense of smell, we can train them for jobs like tracking, rescue, or drug and bomb detection. In one experiment, a line of 12 men followed each other, stepping in each other's footprints. After walking for a distance, each man went left or right to hide. The dog was then asked to find its owner, who was the first man in the line of 12. The dog had no problem finding its owner's scent, even though it had been mixed with that of 11 other people.

Behavior

" Dogs feel very strongly that they should always go with you in the car, in case the need should arise for them to bark violently at nothing right in your ear. "

Dave Barr

Chapter 4
Behavior

Having a badly behaved dog can be a real nightmare. Whether he barks all night, bites the postman or just leaps up at strangers with muddy paws, owning a dog with behavioral problems can make your life a real misery if you're not careful.

So how do you prevent your dog becoming a hound from hell? Well it's all in his training, and if there's one thing to remember, it's that it's never too early to start.

Teaching your dog good behavior should start as soon as you get her home. Puppies are far more receptive to new ideas than older dogs, and while it's not true that you can't teach an old dog new tricks, it certainly does get harder to train dogs as they mature.

Start with a few really simple things, like basic discipline using positive rewards for good behavior. If you give your puppy a nice treat whenever she does something right, such as wee outside, or get off the sofa when she's told to, she'll quickly realize that good behavior leads to nice things happening, and this will make it far easier to train her properly later on.

Lots of people think that the only way to train a dog is to shout at it loudly and give it a smack whenever it does something wrong. This is entirely wrong, and negative training like this should be used as sparingly as possible – and physical discipline should never be required.

It's much more effective to reward the dog whenever he does the right thing, as this motivates the dog to follow your commands and not to misbehave.

Negative commands should only be used when a dog is doing something he really knows he shouldn't be – such as trying to steal a sly sausage off the kitchen table!

Attention is everything for a puppy – it's what they crave – and by giving it to them or denying them, you can easily teach them what you want them to do. For example, puppies that keep playfully biting can be a real pain, and it's important to let them know that it's not acceptable behavior. Do this by stopping any games you are playing as soon as they get too frisky. Simply walk away with a minimum of fuss and come back a few minutes later when they've settled down. If they start to nip again, just get up and go. They will very quickly learn that they have to be good if they want attention.

Rewarding your dog for good behavior is an essential part of the training process. One of the easiest and most effective ways of rewarding a dog is by giving him a little bit of food. There are lots of processed treats available, but these are not always the healthiest option, especially if you're doing lots of training and giving the dog many treats. Instead of using these manufactured treats, why not consider something a bit more healthy, such as a small piece of freshly cooked meat (chicken and liver are real favorites) or even a piece of fruit or veg. It's also a good idea to vary the treats as this will keep your dog's enthusiasm up and also make his diet more varied and healthy.

DID YOU KNOW?

Dogs communicate through body posture and facial expressions. Among the easiest emotions to read are aggression, fear, playfulness, and submission. A dog that is happy and excited will be wagging his tail, prancing around and/or jumping around. A dog that is cowering in the corner is afraid. Here are a few other common canine mannerisms and their meanings:

Play bow: Rear end up, front down, and tail wagging generally means "I want to play."

Tail wagging: Doesn't always mean that the dog is happy or friendly, as is generally assumed. Some dogs also wag their tails when they are scared, agitated or unsure about a situation. Look for other signals to determine the dog's mood.

Rolling over: Generally means the dog is being submissive. Frightened dogs lower their bodies, flatten their ears, tuck their tails, and close their mouths. Whimpering, or even silent, they may roll onto their backs and lie there, belly up.

Tail between legs and ears back: The dog is afraid or feeling apprehensive about something.

Ears perked up: The dog is alert for some reason. During obedience class, it means your dog is paying attention to you and waiting for your next command.

Frontal approach: A dog standing still with hackles raised, ears and tail up and head held high indicates dominance, aggression or a sign of imminent attack. They bare their teeth, and erect the fur along their spine to make themselves look bigger. They may give a menacing growl or a furious bark.

Raised paw: A dog that raises a paw with a bent foreleg is showing submission.

CLICKER TRAINING

One of the best innovations in dog training has been the clicker. These are small plastic devices that make a loud 'click' when you press them. Now you might be wondering how a click can help train a dog – well the answer is in those famous Pavlovian dogs that learnt to salivate whenever they heard a bell. It happened because they were always fed whenever a bell sounded, and so they quickly began to associate the sound of the bell with eating. Later on, they still subconsciously associated the sound of a bell with food, and so they produced saliva, even though there wasn't food around anymore when the bell rang.

It is really easy to use this principle in dog training. All you do is get your dog to associate the sound of the clicker with a reward, such as a biscuit. Whenever he does something good, like sit on command, you click the clicker and give him a treat. After a while, you can start to leave out the treats and just click the clicker, as your dog will have come to associate the sound of the click with a reward – in effect, the click itself has become the reward in the dog's mind.

BASIC COMMANDS

Sit – This is one of the basic commands your dog should obey – and also one of the easiest to teach. A good tip for getting your dog to sit really easily is to take a small treat and hold it above his nose, and then move the treat slightly backwards. As his eyes follow the treat, his back end will naturally drop down towards the ground. As this happens, give him the 'Sit!' command so he associates the action with the word. Once his bottom is down, give him lots of praise and let him eat the treat (and give the clicker a click if you are using that method). Easy!

Recall – If there's one command you really want to work with your dog, it's 'here!'. There is nothing worse than spending hours searching for your dog when he's disappeared in the park, after completely ignoring your desperate shouts, not to mention the dangers of him running onto a road, or chasing other dogs, or people.

Getting your dog to come back on command requires a bit of effort, but if you remember a few important tips, you should have him bounding back to you within a few days.

Firstly, and most importantly, always make sure that, when you begin teaching him to come back, you only ever give the command 'here!' or 'come!' when he is actually coming back to you anyway. If you shout at him to come back when he's racing away in the opposite direction, with his attention focused on a rabbit or ball, he'll ignore you – and worse than that, he won't associate the command with the action of coming back to you. So wait until he's racing back towards you and then shout the command out – that way he'll quickly associate the command with running back to you and will learn to come back whenever you call – well, most of the time anyway!

And secondly, you have to react to your dog's most recent behavior rather than the bad one, as dogs only associate your reaction with what they are doing at that exact moment in time:

You're out in the park and everything is going well. Fred is obeying all your commands and behaving impeccably… just as you are about to head home he suddenly spots a rabbit in the hedge and he's off. You shout yourself hoarse but to no avail – he's gone and there's no sign of him for ages, leaving you fuming impatiently, lead in hand.

Then he suddenly reappears and comes bounding back, tail wagging as if nothing has happened. You are furious though, and give him a piece of your mind for keeping you waiting for so long. He hangs his head in shame and looks thoroughly dejected.

Now you might well think that this was the right thing to do. After all, he's been told off for running away, and looks like he's learnt his lesson. However, that's not quite how Fred will have seen things. In his mind, he was having a great time chasing the rabbit, and then when he finally decided to obey your command and come to you, what did he get for his trouble – a great big telling off!

In these situations, what you have to do, is to grit your teeth and make yourself praise him for coming back to you. Forget the fact that he's been disobeying you for hours, and concentrate on reinforcing his good behavior. It might be hard to do, but if you tell him off, he'll only think that he's in trouble for coming back to you, and that's not going to encourage him to come back again.

BEHAVIORAL PROBLEMS

JUMPING UP

A dog that is constantly jumping up at people can be a real problem – and be a nightmare for you, the owner, and for anyone who comes too close on a muddy day (they always seem to jump up at people when they've just walked through a particularly muddy puddle, and choose the people wearing the most expensive clothes!)

But don't despair if you've got a jumping Jack Russell or a pawing Papillion, here's a simple tip to help you cure this problem.

The thing to do is to ask anyone who has regular contact with her to stick to the following rule: Whenever she jumps up, fold your arms and turn your back on her so she falls back down. Then ask her to sit, and only give her the attention she wants when she's calmly sitting down.

Get as many people as possible to stick to this rule, and she'll soon realize that the best way to get attention is to stay with all four feet on the ground, and not to leap up at people.

OVER-EXCITEMENT

Many dogs get really overexcited whenever the door bell goes, leaping up in a whirlwind of barking and jumping. This can be a bit off-putting for any visitors to the house, not to mention driving you up the wall.

Here are two good tips for dealing with this kind of behavioral problem:

1. Get her used to the doorbell by ringing it regularly throughout the day and opening the door to show that nothing exciting is out there.

2. If she still gets overexcited at the sound of the bell, take her off into the kitchen (or her crate if you have one) for a few minutes of quiet time every time the bell goes. Only let her out to meet the visitor once she's totally calmed down.

SEPARATION ANXIETY

One of the most common problems that drives people and their hounds to pet behaviorists is separation anxiety. This commonly manifests itself as destructive behavior, such as chewing the furniture, or loud, constant barking whenever the dog is left alone.

This can be a really tricky problem to sort out, but, if you catch it early, these tips should help:

1. Get him used to you leaving the house in small stages. First, just pick up your keys and walk towards the door. Do this a few times throughout the day without actually going out and totally ignore the dog even if he barks. After a while, he should get used to this, and you can go a stage further by opening and closing the front door. Finally, leave the house for short periods at a time, making sure you totally ignore any bad behavior. When you come back in, wait until he's completely calmed down before giving him any attention.

2. When you do come back from being out of the house, the worst thing you can do is to make a big fuss of the dog. This only serves to reinforce the drama of you leaving and coming back in the dog's mind, so it's much better to wait until he's really settled down before giving him any attention. This way he'll start to realize that you going out is not such a big deal after all, and he doesn't have to get so wound up by it.

3. Finally, if you're still not getting anywhere, try making a tape or CD with your voice on it – read a book or just talk away, the content doesn't matter. Play the recording on the stereo in the living room and put the dog in the kitchen. This way he'll be tricked into thinking you're still at home when you're out!

EVERYDAY HEALTHCARE

Keeping your beloved dog in good health can be hard work, but if you pay attention to these tips, your dog should stay in the peak of health for many years to come.

PLAY

Playing with your dog is an excellent way of making sure you are really in tune with his body and helps you spot any potential problems early. A bit of hands-on rough and tumble will ensure you are familiar with everything about him, from the texture of his coat, to the length of his nails. Try to run your hands over as much of his body as you can during your playtime sessions, as this is the best way of finding lumps and bumps before they are big enough to see from a distance.

GROOMING

Grooming is not only vital for keeping your dog's coat in tiptop condition, it is also an excellent way of checking your dog over from nose to tail on a regular basis. Anything unusual, such as a lump, swelling or patch of sore skin will be easily spotted and enables you to get some veterinary advice as soon as possible.

Most dogs need occasional grooming – perhaps a good brush once a week and the odd trip to a grooming parlor for a clip and bath – but some breeds need far more coat care. Long-haired breeds, such as Afghan hounds, require daily attention to their coats, and it's well worth asking an experienced groomer for advice with these specialized breeds.

For some dogs, grooming can be a really unpleasant experience. They're poked, prodded, brushed, clipped and even bathed, when they'd much rather be lazing in front of the fire or chasing a squirrel. However, grooming doesn't have to be like this. If you follow a few basic principles early on, dogs can learn to love grooming, and this will make looking after them a whole lot easier.

The key to fun grooming is to associate all the stages of grooming, such as handling, stroking, brushing and clipping, with positive rewards, such as treats. Start by gently rubbing your dog's coat, and give her a treat as you are doing this. Keep repeating this until your dog shows signs of looking forward to being stroked. Then simply repeat this for brushing, clipping, and even bathing, and your dog will soon learn that all these things bring rewards. Within a few weeks she'll be rolling over enthusiastically as soon as you reach for the brush!

If you have a long-haired or shaggy dog, then daily grooming is particularly important, especially in the summer months, thanks to the dangers posed by grass seeds. These innocent-looking awns can be really nasty, because they get trapped in the fur of dogs' ears and feet, and, once there, they can burrow into the skin, and cause horrible infections.

The reason they're so unpleasant is their barbed shape. This means that, once they've pierced the skin, they can only move in one direction – deeper in. As the dog moves, the seed will gradually work its way into the foot or ear, and cause a painful swelling filled with infection. Often, the first time a dog owner will know of this is when the dog goes lame and is constantly licking his foot, or his ear develops a foul smell.

There is a way of preventing grass seed problems though, and that is to check your dog's ears and feet thoroughly after every walk in grassy areas in summer. It's mainly spaniels and terriers that suffer from this problem, but any dog with hairy ears or feet should be checked. It's well worth the effort, as it could save your dog from a very nasty infection – and you from a big vet bill!

NAILS

There's a common misconception amongst many dog owners that all dogs need their nails clipped on a regular basis. In fact, most active dogs that walk at least some of the time on hard surfaces, like roads, generally never need their nails doing. It's usually older dogs or those who exercise solely on grass who need the occasional trim, but here's a tip that will help you decide whether your dog's nails need attention – and it's all to do with letters…

A nail of the perfect length should look like a slightly long letter 'r' (where the end of the pad is the straight stem of the letter, and curved top represents the nail). Nails that are overgrown start to look more like a letter 'b', as the nail grows round and heads back towards the pad. The correct length is when the nail forms a quarter circle when viewed from the side – any longer than this, and you should give the nails a trim – or pop down to your vet for a quick pedicure!

Half of the battle of nail clipping can be won by choosing the right nail clippers for your dog. Cheap, flimsy clippers can make the whole job much more difficult and uncomfortable for the dog, and are usually a false economy. Invest in a good, solid pair of clippers, and buy ones that are suitable for the size of your dog. The most effective clippers are those that encircle the nail and act like a guillotine. Clippers that are open-ended tend to squeeze the nail painfully before they cut, and should be avoided.

Lots of dogs hate having their nails clipped and even just the sight of the clippers can send them into an anxious frenzy. The best way to avoid this kind of drama at nail-trimming time is to get the dog accustomed to the clippers gradually over several weeks. It helps if you can do this when she is as young as possible, but older dogs can also be helped to overcome a fear of nail clipping using the same principle.

All you need to do is get her to associate everything about nail clipping with good things. So start by playing with her feet and giving her a treat. Then gradually bring the clippers in and have them in you hands as you touch her feet (but don't clip yet), again giving her treats as you do so. Then finally, after a few weeks of repeating this several times a day, gently start trimming the very ends of her nails and giving her a treat as you do so.

Follow this advice, and your dog should never have a problem with having her nails trimmed.

The main danger with cutting nails is cutting them too short and hitting the quick. The quick is the red part of the nail that is full of nerves and blood vessels, and if you cut into this area it is really painful for the dog, and can cause some quite unpleasant bleeding, which can be hard to stop.

The best tip for avoiding this is to identify the quick and make sure you cut the nail at least 3 or 4 mm below the end of it. In dogs with light-colored nails, this is usually pretty easy as the quick is visible as the red area at the top of the nail. Black nails are much harder, because it is impossible to see the quick. What you should do with these nails is line the clippers up with the bottom of the pad, and check that your cut will leave a full quarter circle of nail when you look side on. If in doubt, leave an extra few millimeters – it's not worth taking the risk of hitting the quick.

DENTAL HYGIENE

Having a big slobbery kiss from your dog can be a lovely sign of affection – but if his mouth is full of rotten teeth, the experience can be a whole lot less enjoyable! And, of course, there are more serious consequences if your dog has bad teeth. Dental problems can be very painful, put your dog off his food, and even cause infections to spread to other parts of the body via the bloodstream.

Just like ourselves, regular brushing is the most important preventative health measure for dogs' teeth. We all brush our teeth every day, but, unfortunately, not all dog owners are as diligent when it comes to their dog's teeth – which can lead to some very unpleasant long term consequences. Just imagine what your teeth would be like in a few years' time if you never brushed them – pretty unpleasant! In fact, not brushing is one of the big reasons why so many dogs have rotten teeth. Food and bacteria collect on the teeth, leading to tartar build up and dental decay.

Brushing your dog's teeth is not very hard, and it's well worth getting into a regular routine, where you give his teeth a good cleaning every day. You must use a special soft doggy toothbrush and toothpaste made for dogs. There are lots of lovely flavors available, like beef and chicken, and they are formulated so as to be safe for the dog to swallow (as it's hard to ask a dog to rinse and spit!)

As with all new things, get your dog used to having his teeth brushed gradually, using lots of treats and rewards for good behavior. Brush using a circular motion with the tip of the brush at 45 degrees to the teeth, and work your way around all of his teeth.

You might wonder what happens to all the wild dogs, wolves and foxes that have survived quite happily for thousands of years without so much as a whiff of toothpaste – do they all have horrible teeth, or could it be that they've got a different way of keeping their teeth clean?

The answer lies in the diet of these wild canines. They're all scavengers and spend a lot of time chewing over the carcasses of other animals and – most importantly – grinding their teeth on the bones. This action of gnawing away on hard bones works wonders for their teeth, as it cleans away any food scraps and bacteria, just like brushing does.

It's not just wild dogs who can keep their teeth clean by gnawing bones. Domestic dogs love chewing bones and it's a great way of preventing dental problems. I recommend giving all dogs a good bone to chew on at least once a month. Simply pop down to your butcher and ask for a nice meaty bone – and your dog will spend hours happily chewing away, and his teeth will be as clean as a whistle by the time he's finished!

There's just one really important thing to remember about bones though, and that is that the bone *must* be raw. Cooked bones are dangerous because they splinter and leave sharp fragments.

EAR PROBLEMS

If I had a pound for every dog on the planet who suffered from bad ears, I'd be a rich vet indeed. Ear infections are one of the most common problems affecting dogs, and there are all sorts of causes, from tiny mites to waxy infections.

However, not all dogs suffer from ear disease, and the reason why some do and some don't usually comes down to the shape of their ear, and the amount of hair around the ear opening. Dogs like spaniels, which have very hairy ears that flop down by the sides of their head, tend to have far more trouble with ear infections than short-haired dogs with pointy ears. This is because the thick fur and floppy ears tend to prevent air circulating in and out of the ear, making them perfect for bacteria to breed in.

To help prevent ear infections in dogs with hairy ears, the best thing to do is pluck as much hair as you can out of the ear. Arm yourself with a pair of tweezers and grab hold of the hairs poking out of the ear canal in little clumps – then pull with a swift tug. You should be able to pluck out most of the hair this way, and if you only pull a few hairs at a time, it shouldn't be too uncomfortable for the dog. If he really doesn't like it, you might want to get your groomer or vet to do it for you.

If your dog has waxy ears, it's important to clean them out effectively or infection is likely to set in. The best thing to use is a proper ear cleaner, which you can get from your vet or pet shop.

My top tip for cleaning out a waxy ear is to hold the tip of your dog's ear in one hand and hold it up vertically. This will open the ear canal up, and allow you to pour a generous amount of cleaner down the ear. Then gently massage the ear canal with your other hand to loosen the wax, before wiping it out with a ball of cotton wool.

A dog's ear canal goes straight down before turning a corner and heading in towards his head. At the end of this horizontal part is the delicate ear drum, and you must be really careful not to damage this when you are cleaning your dog's ears. Most problems occur when people use cotton wool buds, because these can reach all the way down to the ear drum. However, there is a way of making sure you never cause any problems, even if you are using buds.

The tip is to hold the ear tip up nice and high, and push the cotton bud down parallel to the ear and the side of his head. When it reaches the bottom of the vertical part of the ear canal, you will safely hit the corner of the canal not the ear drum. You can be quite vigorous using this method, as there is no way you will hit the ear drum as long as you keep the cotton bud parallel to his head.

DID YOU KNOW?

A dog's ear is very sensitive, full of sensory nerves that help to preserve hearing. Never blow into a dog's ear, even gently, this can hurt a dog. It's not the actual act of wind, but the frequency at which you blow. It's like running your fingernails down a blackboard, amplified hundreds of times.

DID YOU KNOW?

Using their swiveling ears like radar dishes, experiments have shown that dogs can locate the source of a sound in 6/100ths of a second.

HEALTHCARE DIARY

Confused by all the healthcare tips? Well don't be – here's a summary of what you should be doing every day, week and month to keep your dog in great shape:

Every day:

- Brush teeth
- A good session of hands-on play, checking all over for any lumps or bumps
- Check feet and ears for grass seeds after walks in the summer
- Check eyes for discharges and redness
- Groom long-haired breeds

Every week:

- Check ears for signs of wax
- Groom
- Give dental chew to keep teeth clean
- Check coat carefully for fleas

Every month:

- Check nails and trim if necessary
- Check ears and pluck away any overgrowing fur
- Give big raw bone or pig's ear to chew on
- Examine teeth and consider a veterinary opinion if in doubt
- Treat for fleas (exact frequency depends on the product being used)

Every three months:

- Worm with a good quality worming tablet

Every year:

- Annual checkup and vaccinations at your vet

Feeding Your Dog

" I've seen a look in dogs' eyes, a quickly vanishing look of amazed contempt, and I am convinced that basically dogs think humans are nuts. "

John Steinbeck

Chapter 5

Feeding Your Dog

There's a well-known saying 'you are what you eat', and this applies just as much to your dog as to yourself. Get your dog's food wrong and he could end up with some serious health problems, so it's well worth making sure your dog has a healthy diet that suits his individual requirements.

When thinking about the food your dog eats, it's well worth bearing in mind the fact that all modern domestic dogs are descended from wolves and wild dogs. These ancient animals were omnivorous scavengers – in other words, they ate anything and everything they could get their teeth into! The main part of their diet would have been the remains of carcasses left behind by predators, so bones, meat, and vegetable matter from the animal's stomach would have all been chewed up by these scavenging canines.

Now I'm not for a moment suggesting that you try and feed your pet dog on anything like this kind of diet, but it is important that all the key ingredients and nutrients from this wild diet are present in your modern dog's dinner. Your dog needs this mix of vegetable matter and meat in order to stay healthy, and there are several different ways to achieve this kind of balanced diet.

COMPLETE DIETS

The easiest way of feeding your dog the right mix of nutrients is to give her one of the complete foods available. These are either available as wet foods (tins, trays or pouches), or as dried kibbles. Each chunk of the wet food, or biscuit of the dried diets, is specially formulated to contain all the protein, fat, carbohydrate, vitamins and minerals your dog needs.

As with most things in life, you really get what you pay for with complete dog foods. It's all very well saving money by buying the cheapest food from the supermarket, but just remember that the reason it costs so little is that it's made from the very cheapest ingredients. This can include such delicacies as feathers, feet and other animal by-products, and usually very little real meat.

While foods like this will generally contain all the basic nutrients your dog needs, they will also contain a lot of artificial preservatives, flavors and colors (in order to disguise the taste of all those chicken feet and feathers!). They are not good for the long term health of your dog, and are best avoided if at all possible.

At the other end of the dog food spectrum are premium and super-premium complete diets. These are a lot more expensive than the cheaper brands, but are much better for your dog. The best brands don't use any artificial chemicals or animal by-products, just real meat protein and a healthy carbohydrate source, such as brown rice. If your budget will stretch to one of these top brands, it's well worth the extra cost, as your dog is much more likely to live a happier and healthier life as a result.

RAW FEEDING

Some people recommend that dogs should be fed on a diet of raw meat and bones, but whilst this sounds like a very good idea in principle, my tip is to stick to properly cooked food. The main reason is food hygiene. Whilst dogs do have very sturdy digestive systems, and can cope with far more unpleasant bacteria in their food than we can, there still exists a risk that raw food will cause problems, either through bacteria like salmonella, or parasites like tapeworm cysts. And there's also a risk to human health if raw meat is being prepared and fed in the kitchen.

Cooking meat protects your dog from these risks, and also aids the digestibility of the food and reduces the fat content. It does have some negative effects, such as reducing the levels of some nutrients, but this will not be in any way significant if your dog is being fed primarily on a complete food.

The main exception is raw bones. Chewing on uncooked bones is great for your dog's overall health, as they keep his teeth clean as well as providing loads of minerals to keep his bones strong. Never feed him cooked bones, as these can splinter and cause nasty internal problems.

DID YOU KNOW?

Dogs have far fewer taste buds than people – they have about 1,700 on their tongues, while we humans have about 9,000 – and it is the smell that initially attracts them to a particular food.

HOME-COOKING

An alternative to feeding just complete foods is to add in some home-cooked recipes. And although cooking for your dog everyday is not practical for most people – and isn't generally recommended unless you are very knowledgeable about nutrition, as it's easy to cause problems if you don't feed them a well-balanced diet – a weekly meal of fresh meat and veg is a great way of treating your dog and giving him some really healthy, fresh food in his diet.

However, before you head off into the kitchen and start cooking for your dog, there are some really important things to bear in mind. Firstly, and most importantly, you have to always remember that you are cooking for a dog and not for a person. Dogs and people have different nutritional needs and some foods that are fine for people can be dangerous to dogs – and vice versa. And don't forget that some flavors you might find horrible will be the ones that your dog absolutely loves, so be prepared to hold your nose and work through the smell barrier for your dog!

Secondly, some of the recipes use an ingredient called brewer's yeast, which you might not be aware of. It's basically the pasteurized residue of commercial brewed beer and it's packed full of all sorts of nutrients, including protein and vitamins. You can buy it in powder or tablet form from your local health store, and it's well worth getting a jar if you're keen on following a few of these recipes.

And finally, some tips on what you can and can't use in recipes for dogs. The most important foods to avoid are:

- Tomatoes – a small amount of ripe tomato is unlikely to cause any problems, but green tomatoes can cause serious stomach upsets and even heart problems, so it's best to avoid them.

- Onions (and garlic) – can cause blood problems including anaemia. Again, small amounts are very unlikely to cause any problems, but, to be on the safe side, I only use small amounts of garlic and very little onion in my recipes.

- Grapes and raisins – both can cause very serious illness, including kidney problems, and large amounts have been known to be fatal to dogs, so avoid wherever possible.

- Chocolate – one of the ingredients of chocolate, theobromine, is related to caffeine, and some dogs react very badly to it, showing signs like hyper-excitability, increased heart rate and muscle tremors. Dark chocolates contain the highest levels of theobromine, but I'd advise keeping all chocolate away from dogs.

- Mushrooms – best avoided as some dogs will not tolerate mushrooms well and they can cause serious toxicity.

On the other side of the equation, there are a few rather surprising ingredients that are really healthy for your dog, such as:

- Fruit – in the wild, dogs would have scavenged windfall fruit as well as digesting the remains of fruit eaten by other animals when they pick over the carcass, so giving your dog fruit is not as strange as it might sound. Fresh fruit is packed full of antioxidants, vitamins and all sorts of other healthy nutrients, so it's great for keeping your dog in top condition. The only tricky part is persuading him that he really does want to eat fruit – which is where some of my more ingenious recipes involving fruit and liver come in!

- Yoghurt – this is a great source of protein, calcium and vitamins, and is particularly good for dogs with diarrhea, thanks to the probiotics it contains.

- Cottage cheese – another surprisingly healthy dairy food, which is great for growing puppies and lactating bitches.

- Raw Bones – there are a lot of scare stories about feeding bones to your dog, but, in fact, as long as they aren't cooked, they are really safe and very good for your dog in many ways (never feed cooked bones as these will splinter and cause lots of trouble). Raw bones provide an excellent source of minerals such as calcium, and as well as keeping your dog's teeth clean, they keep him entertained for hours on end. So don't be afraid to ask your butcher for a good big juicy marrowbone every now and then – your dog will love you for it!

EVERYDAY MEALS

CHICKEN AND RICE

This dish combines one of the healthiest proteins available – chicken – with rice, which is an easily digestible carbohydrate and a mixture of veg that provides lots of vitamins and minerals. It's great for all dogs, including those with sensitive digestions and older dogs.

It's ideal for freezing, so you can store it in single-serving sized bags, then simply de-frost a tasty and healthy meal the next time you want to give your dog something special.

For a couple of medium dog portions, you'll need:

- 225g chicken mince

- 200g rice (preferably brown)

- 1 small carrot, finely grated

- 150g fresh peas

- 1 tsp yeast extract

Boil the rice in a large pan of boiling water. When the rice is almost cooked (1-2 minutes away), drop the grated carrot and peas into the water and let it simmer until the rice is done. This makes the veg much more digestible, without losing all of its goodness. When the rice is cooked, drain well.

Meanwhile, fry the mince for a few minutes until it is browned – you shouldn't need to add any oil as there is plenty of fat in the mince – and add it to the rice. Finally, mix in the yeast extract and serve once cooled.

FISHY DELIGHT

Fish is a great source of healthy protein for your dog, and it also contains high levels of omega-3 oils, which are great for the heart. On the downside, raw fish can interfere with the uptake of some vitamins, so it's best avoided.

This simple recipe makes enough for several servings and has an extra boost of calcium from the ground egg shells, which makes it ideal for young growing dogs and whelping bitches, as well as being a good everyday dish.

- 500g (1 lb) boneless white fish

- 1 cup rice (brown if possible)

- 1 tin oily fish (sardines or pilchards)

- 3 eggs

- 1 carrot (grated)

Steam the fish (or boil if you prefer) for about 20 minutes – until it is flaky and cooked through. At the same time, cook the rice according to the instructions on the packet, and hard-boil the eggs. Put the grated carrot into the rice water a couple of minutes before it's cooked, just to make it more digestible.

Once the fish, rice and carrot are cooked, mix them all together in a large bowl. Take the shell off the eggs – but don't throw it away – and break up the eggs into small chunks, then mix them into the fish and rice mixture. Scoop up the shell and grind it into as fine a powder as you can with a pestle and mortar (or rolling pin if it's all you've got), adding about a teaspoon into the mix. The grittiness of the calcium in the shell helps clean your dog's teeth as he eats.

Finally, pour in the tinned fish, complete with all the oil, and mix everything together thoroughly. Sprinkle a little parsley over the top if you fancy – but don't expect the dog to take any notice – it'll get wolfed down with the rest of it!

LAMB STEW WITH CRUNCHY CROUTONS

There's nothing quite like this hearty stew for warming the inner dog after he's been out for a long winter walk. It's full of healthy veg and low in fat and salt, which makes it another great all-rounder. Best served warm, on a cold day.

To make enough for a pack of hungry hounds, you need:

- 250g lamb or mutton, diced

- 1 carrot

- 1 potato

- 1 apple

- 1 cup stale bread

This is one of the easiest recipes around. Simply cover the lamb with cold water in a large pan, bring to the boil and simmer for 1 hour. While this is bubbling away, chop up the carrots, potatoes and apples into rough chunks, and break up the bread into small pieces. Cook the bread in a low oven for half an hour, so that it is crisp but not burnt.

Add the carrot, potato and apple to the lamb after an hour, and simmer it all together for about 7-8 minutes – until the veg are partially cooked but still firm. Then allow to cool but serve while it is still warm. Mix in the bread croutons at the last minute so they stay crunchy.

TREATS

Like it or not, treats are a part of most dogs' diets and they can be very helpful for training and rewards. However, not all treats are as good for a dog's physical health as they are for their behavior, and it's easy to cause weight gain and other health problems by using unhealthy treats.

These recipes are designed to be both super-tasty and healthy as well, so as long as you are sensible with your rewards, you don't have to worry that your treats are contributing to his waistline.

LIVER AND BACON CHEWS

In my mind, there are few smells as appealing as that of bacon gently crisping in a pan. And it's not just me that thinks like this – every dog I've ever known, also loves bacon, which is why these lovely chewy treats are such a winner.

They're made of crunchy pieces of bacon in a chewy dough made from liver, egg and flour, and they are brilliant as training bribes (my dog learnt how to shake hands in one afternoon with a tray of these treats!).

So cook up a batch and keep them to hand for an occasional reward or training titbit.

For a decent sized batch, you will need:

- 225g liver

- 1 egg

- 1 cup flour

- ¼ teaspoon oregano

- 2 rashers bacon

Fry the bacon until just crisp, and then allow it to cool before cutting it up into tiny pieces. Keep the fat from the cooking as you'll need that in a minute.

Next, put the liver into the blender and whiz it until it forms a thick red sludge. Pour in the fat from the frying pan (wait until it has cooled a little), break in the egg and sprinkle in the oregano. Fire up the blender again and continue to mix for a few seconds, until it forms a nice, uniform paste. Then pour it into a large mixing bowl and add in the bacon and mix well.

Finally, mix in the flour to form a thick dough, which you can roll out and divide into grape-sized pieces. Place these on a well-greased baking tray and cook in a moderate oven for half an hour.

FRUIT SHAKE

It might surprise you, but, in the wild, dogs would eat quite a lot of fruit. This comes from eating the remains of other animals that have themselves eaten fruit, and from picking up windfalls. It provides a great supply of energy in the form of readily available fruit sugars, as well as all the vitamins and antioxidants we associate with fruit.

So this recipe, which is stuffed full of the goodness of raw fruit, is one of the healthiest in the book and the addition of a bit of yoghurt also adds to its healthy qualities and makes it more palatable.

Some dogs will lap this up on its own, but, for the average, fast-food loving hound, you might need to pour it over his everyday dinner to get the goodness down him.

For enough for several portions, you'll need:

- 1 banana

- 1 apple

- A few strawberries

- 1 orange

- 1 small pot of yoghurt (125ml)

Put the peeled banana (watch out where you put the skin…), apple and strawberries into a blender and whiz them up until they are well and truly puréed. Pour into a bowl and add in the peeled and chopped up orange. Finally, mix in the yoghurt and give it a good stir.

Try this out but if he turns his nose up, you can try either pouring it over his dried dog kibbles, or adding half a tin of wet meaty dog food to the shake mixture.

MEALS FOR SPECIAL OCCASIONS

We all like to mark a special occasion with some kind of feast, whether it's a meal down the pub on your birthday, or a romantic dinner for two on Valentine's Day. But what about our four-legged friends? Well here are a few ideas for some meals that will let your best friend know how much he's loved on those special days.

POOCH PIZZA

Ideal for a doggy birthday, this tasty pizza is healthy thanks to the layer of spinach, which provides iron and vitamins, and the low-fat turkey mince on top. The base is made from your dog's normal dried food, so it's got all the goodness he normally gets every day, as well as the extra tasty topping.

For one medium dog-sized pizza, you'll need:

- 100g dried dog kibble

- 50g plain flour

- 30g butter or margarine

- 100g spinach, finely chopped

- 100g turkey mince

- 50g grated cheddar cheese

Firstly, you need to grind up the dried biscuits into a fine powder using a blender. Then moisten the kibble powder with enough warm water to make it into a really moist and gooey mess. Leave it to stand for ten minutes, and add more water if you need to, as the kibble absorbs a lot of water.

Next, add in the flour and slightly melted butter, and mix it all together to form a thick dough. It should firm up into a nice dry ball you can roll out on a floured surface until it's about ¼ inch thick.

For the topping, you need to fry up the turkey mince for five minutes or so and then mix it together with the finely chopped spinach. Cover the base with this mixture and, finally, sprinkle on the grated cheese.

Cook in a moderate oven for 20-25 minutes – until the top is golden brown. Allow to cool thoroughly and then slice into wedges before serving.

TURKEY AND TRIMMINGS CHRISTMAS BALLS

This is a really quick and easy recipe for a cracking Christmas dinner for your dog. It is really tasty but also a much healthier option than feeding scraps from your Christmas dinner table. It only takes about 20 minutes to prepare and about half an hour in the oven, alongside your turkey.

All the dogs at my surgery (well and ill!) loved this recipe – and the best thing is you'll have most of the ingredients in the fridge ready for your big meal anyway, so it's no real effort to make.

- 250g turkey mince

- A couple of medium potatoes (around 350g)

- 1 good sized carrot (around 200g)

- A handful of sprouts (about 250g)

- ½ teaspoon yeast extract

- 1 teaspoon cranberry sauce

- Gravy from your Christmas dinner

Firstly, boil the potatoes and sprouts for 10-15 minutes until well-cooked. Then drain them and set about them with a masher until they form a rough and sticky mash.

Meanwhile, heat up a frying pan and gently brown the mince. You don't need any oil as there is plenty of fat in the meat. Once the mince is cooked through, mix it into the mash, add in the cranberry sauce (great for urinary health), and, finally, just add a healthy dose of B vitamins and a bit of extra meatiness to the flavor by stirring in the yeast extract.

While the mixture is cooling down, grease a baking tray – and then it's time to get your hands dirty! Form the sticky mix into walnut-sized balls and smooth them off, before placing them on the baking tray.

Pop the tray into a moderate oven for half an hour or so – until the balls are nicely crisp and brown – and then take them out and let them stand for at least twenty minutes to cool down. Then arrange them in the dog's bowl, pour a little gravy over and serve.

BIRTHDAY CAKE

What better way to celebrate the dog's big day than with a big, tasty cake? However, you can't just bake a normal human cake – it'll be too rich and is likely to upset the dog's digestive tract – and that's the last thing you want on the dog's birthday! So here's a recipe for a healthy doggy birthday cake that will put a smile on the dog's face, and won't cause trouble.

To make a cake big enough for 3 or 4 dogs, you'll need:

- 250g beef mince

- 1 grated carrot

- 75g oatmeal

- 75g flour

- 30g butter

- 3 eggs

- Yoghurt

- 2 rashers of bacon

Fry the mince until brown, add in the grated carrot and continue to cook gently for a few minutes. Meanwhile, mix together the flour and oatmeal and rub in the butter. Beat in the eggs to form a sticky paste, and then add in the mince and carrot, complete with any juice from the pan. Knead the mixture together and press it into a well-greased cake tin. Cook for 30 minutes in a moderate oven and then turn out and allow to cool.

Grill the bacon until crisp and then cut it up into small pieces. Cover the cake with yoghurt and sprinkle on the bacon pieces.

MEALS TO SHARE

Lots of dogs waddle into my surgery after a lifetime of titbits and leftovers. This kind of diet almost invariably leads to weight problems, which, in turn, cause diseases such as diabetes, heart and liver disease, as well as making conditions such as arthritis much worse. So feeding your dog from your plate is a bad thing then? Well not necessarily, these recipes are specially designed to be healthy for you and for the dog, so you can share a meal together every now and then.

Just one word of warning here – always eat your meal before you give the dog his portion, otherwise he'll start to think he's the top dog and that will lead to behavioral problems.

HADDOCK AND CORIANDER FISH CAKES WITH RICE

I must admit to having a real soft spot for fish cakes, and one of the nurses at the surgery has a dog who feels the same. I cook up a dish of these in the evening, and then take a left-over cake and a bit of rice into the surgery for her dog the next day. The first time I tried this recipe, I included a bit of Thai curry paste, which I loved – but the dog didn't agree. Since then, I've left this out, and we're both very happy with the recipe!

To make enough for 4 (including the dog!) you'll need:

- 1 kg potatoes

- 400g haddock fillet

- 300ml milk

- 4 tablespoons chopped coriander

- 4 tablespoons plain flour

- 1 egg, beaten

- 75g breadcrumbs

- 2 tablespoons oil

Boil the potatoes for about 15 minutes, until they are nice and soft. Meanwhile, put the fish in a large saucepan and cover with the milk. Bring to the boil and then immediately turn off the heat and allow to cook in the juices for five minutes, by which time it should be nice and flaky. Remove from the milk and discard the skin and bones.

Mash the potatoes and add in the coriander and flaked fish. Mix well and form into 8 cakes. Dip each cake in the beaten egg and coat with breadcrumbs. Heat the oil in a frying pan and cook the cakes for about 5 minutes, turning halfway through. Drain with kitchen paper to absorb the oil and serve on a bed of rice.

SAUSAGE AND LENTIL CASSEROLE

A great dish for you and the dog to share on a cold winter's evening after a long walk. Lentils are not a bad food for dogs, but they are not totally nutritionally balanced (and can cause wind!) so this is a dish best fed occasionally rather than every day. Reserve it for a particularly wet and cold evening when you both need cheering up with something warm and tasty.

To make enough for you, the dog, and a couple of friends, you will need:

- 6 sausages

- 1 teaspoon olive oil

- 1 small leek, finely chopped

- 2 garlic cloves, crushed

- 150g Puy lentils

- 1 pint (600ml) chicken stock

- 1 teaspoon balsamic vinegar

- 3 tablespoons chopped parsley

- Salt and pepper

Fry the sausages in the olive oil for 7 or 8 minutes until browned all the way around. Then add in the chopped leek and garlic and cook for a further 5 minutes.

Next, add in the lentils and hot stock. Bring to the boil and simmer gently for 45 minutes, until the lentils are tender and most of the stock has been absorbed. Finally, add in the vinegar and parsley, and season with salt and pepper for taste.

Eat yours while it's still piping hot, but make the dog wait until it has cooled down before spooning out a couple of sausages and sauce into his bowl.

SPECIAL MEALS

There are times in your dog's life when he might need some special attention to his diet – perhaps he's under the weather and needs a healthy boost, or maybe he's just got a bit too big around the middle and would benefit from some low-calorie treats to help get him back into shape.

These recipes are specially designed to address particular problems, so if your dog isn't quite right, have a look through this section and see if there's a recipe that fits the bill.

CHICKEN SOUP – FOR THE SICKLY DOG

This recipe is full of goodness from the chicken and veg, and it's easily eaten and digested. If your dog is a bit below par, or recovering from something more serious, this recipe is ideal and guaranteed to get him back on the road to recovery.

You'll need:

- 2 chicken drumsticks

- 1 carrot

- 1 potato

- 1 teaspoon parsley

- 1 stock cube

It's really easy this one – just cover the chicken and chopped up veg with boiling water and simmer on a low heat for thirty minutes. Then fish out the chicken, remove the bones and return the meat to the pan. Sprinkle in the parsley and allow to cool. Best served slightly warm, with natural dried food sprinkled in as croutons.

YOGHURT CHICKEN AND RICE – FOR THE DOG WITH DIARRHEA

There are lots of possible causes of diarrhea, ranging from nasty infections to dietary insensitivities, but the treatment often has one thing in common – a period of starvation (often 24 hours) followed by the use of a really bland diet for a few days. This regime is often sufficient to sort out most mild cases of diarrhea, and it's a sensible first step to consider rather than rushing to the vet straight away (obviously, if this doesn't do the trick, or the dog is really unwell, you should get him straight to the surgery for a proper check over).

This recipe is particularly good because both chicken and rice are very easily digested and unlikely to irritate the bowel, and the live yoghurt provides probiotics that help to restore the correct balance of good bacteria in the gut.

For a couple of average dog portions, you'll need:

- 200g chicken mince

- ½ cup of rice (preferably brown)

- Plain, live yoghurt

Add the rice and the mince to a large pan of boiling water. Cooking them together in this way means the flavor of the meat soaks deep into the rice, making it much more palatable (which is important for such a bland meal).

When the rice is cooked, drain away the water and allow the mixture to cool.

For each serving, mix with a tablespoon of yoghurt (for a Labrador-sized dog).

LOW-FAT TREATS

If the dog is looking a little tubby around the middle, but he lives for his daily treat (or two), here's a recipe for some biscuits that will keep him satisfied, but won't pile on quite so many pounds.

- ½ pint (250ml) hot water

- 1 beef stock cube

- 2 tablespoons olive oil

- 4 cups whole wheat flour

- 1 stick celery, finely chopped

- 1 carrot, grated

Dissolve the stock cube in the hot water and add to the flour and vegetables in a large mixing bowl. Add the stock gradually to form a thick dough, which you can roll out on a well-floured surface until it is about 1cm thick. Then cut out small biscuit shapes using a knife or the end of an apple corer. Try to make the biscuits a little bit smaller than normal – every little helps when it comes to cutting down the calories!

Place the biscuits on a greased baking tray and cook in a moderate oven for about half an hour. Allow to cool and then ration with steely determination! (Store in the fridge in an airtight container for several weeks)

BEEFY RICE – FOR THE DIABETIC DOG

If your dog has been diagnosed with diabetes, you'll be aware of the importance of getting her diet just right. Diabetes is a disease of the

" If you can look at a dog and not feel vicarious excitement and affection, you must be a cat. "

Anon

sugar control system in the body, and is generally treated in dogs by using injections of insulin, which reduces the level of sugar in the blood. These injections are only half the story, though, as diet is just as crucial in keeping good control of the amount of sugar in the system.

The ideal diet for a diabetic dog will contain lots of so-called 'complex carbohydrates' such as starch, and also plenty of fiber, while having low levels of simple sugars. This reduces the peaks and troughs of sugar in the blood by releasing energy gradually through the day.

The best way of getting this kind of diet right is to feed a specially formulated commercial diet from your vet. But that doesn't mean you can't treat her to the occasional home-cooked meal. As long as you stick to recipes like this one, which are low in sugar and high in starch and fiber, you can definitely cook up something tasty once a week or so, just to add a little variety to her life.

This basic diabetes recipe provides approximately 50% complex carbohydrates, which is ideal:

- 750ml water

- 1 stock cube

- 450g lean beef, cubed

- 1 carrot, grated

- 1 stick of celery, finely chopped

- 100g broccoli, finely chopped

- 100g spinach

- 150g brown rice

Boil up the water and dissolve the stock cube in it. Then drop in the beef and simmer for about twenty minutes. Fish out the beef once cooked and set it aside in a large bowl with the grated and finely chopped veg. Put the rice into the boiling stock and cook for about 30 minutes until tender (less if you are using white rice).

Then drain any remaining water off the rice and pour the rice over the veg and meat, mixing well. The hot, moist rice will effectively steam the grated veggies, so they can be easily digested, but don't lose any nutrients.

Allow this mixture to cool and then feed. It can be frozen in single serving bags, so you can defrost one every week or so.

VENISON, RABBIT OR DUCK AND POTATO – THE HYPOALLERGENIC DIET

Food intolerances and allergies are relatively common in dogs and can be serious problems. Intolerances are when the dog can't digest a certain food, such as milk, whereas allergies are more serious and involve nasty reactions to food, including itching skin and diarrhea.

If your dog has a food intolerance or allergy, your vet will probably recommend a suitable hypoallergenic diet, which is free of the particular foods your dog reacts to. Whilst it is ideal to stick to this food as much as you can, there is nothing wrong with cooking a tasty meal for your dog every now and then, as long as it is also free of whatever is causing your dog's symptoms.

This recipe is designed to suit most intolerant or allergic dogs, but it's important to check with your vet before using this, or any recipe, to make sure it won't cause problems.

For enough for several meals (it's easily freezable), you will need:

- 450g venison, rabbit or duck – minced*

- 450g potatoes

- 2 eggs

- 2 carrots

* Most dogs will be fine on venison, rabbit or duck, but obviously avoid any of these if your vet advises that your dog could be allergic or intolerant to them.

Dice the potatoes and carrots, boil them until tender and then drain and mash together. Meanwhile, hardboil the eggs and, when done (8 minutes), crush up one of the shells and add the fine powder, plus both eggs, to the potato mash.

Fry the minced meat until cooked through, using a little olive oil if necessary, and then add to the mash and mix in thoroughly.

BALANCED CHICKEN AND RICE
– FOR DOGS WITH KIDNEY OR LIVER DISEASE

As dogs get older, many will suffer from liver and/or kidney disease, with symptoms ranging from weight loss to vomiting and collapse. Treating these two problems can be very tricky, and diet is an essential part of helping your dog cope. Once your dog has been diagnosed as suffering from liver or kidney disease, your vet may well recommend a special prescription diet for him, which contains the ideal levels of nutrients he needs to limit the deterioration of the condition.

However, just because he's on this special diet, it doesn't necessarily mean that home cooking is out of the window. It is possible to cook the occasional special meal for your dog, as long as you stick to a recipe that meets the following requirements:

- Slightly reduced protein level

- Good quality protein – fish and chicken are ideal

- Low phosphorus – so avoid dairy foods and rich deep green veg, like spinach

- High moisture content

This recipe provides a tasty alternative to the prescription foods for liver and kidney disease, and is ideal as a once-a-week treat:

You will need:

- 100g brown rice

- 200g chicken mince

- 1 carrot, grated

- 1 teaspoon calcium carbonate (from your health food shop)

- 1 multivitamin tablet

Simply boil up the rice until almost cooked (about 25 minutes) and then drop in the grated carrot and continue to simmer until the rice is tender. Meanwhile, brown the mince in a frying pan (without oil) until cooked through.

When the rice is cooked, drain away the water and add in the mince. Crush up the multivitamin and add it with the calcium to the mix.

Traveling With Your Dog

" Number one way life would be different if dogs ran the world: All motorists must drive with head out window. "

David Letterman

Chapter 6
Traveling With Your Dog

It's only natural that, when we go on vacation, we would want to take our furry friends too. Where once that would have been impossible because of quarantine laws, these days things have moved on and it can often be the case of the dog can come too.

In fact, doggy travel has become so common that dogs even have their own Pet Passports, through the Pet Travel Scheme (PETS).

TIP: Before deciding whether your dog should come along, ask yourself if they will genuinely be happier with you or would they be better off either at home being looked after by friends or family or in a boarding kennel?

WHAT IS A PET PASSPORT?

For years, if pet owners wanted to take their dogs abroad, they were forced to place them in quarantine for six months and sometimes longer. This was to stop the spread of rabies.

Not only was quarantine expensive (owners had to pay), there were also grave concerns about animals being away from their owners and home comforts for months on end. Dogs could become very traumatized.

It was as the result of people being unhappy with their healthy pets being placed in quarantine, that the Pet Travel Scheme came about with the introduction of Pet Passports.

Pet Passports allow dogs, cats and, would you believe it, ferrets, to travel between member countries (including the USA, UK and Canada) without undergoing quarantine first. You can get one from your vet, along with details of how the scheme works.

Countries that are approved for the Pet Travel Scheme are done so because they have a low rabies risk (in the case of the UK, it has been rabies free for many years).

For more information on the Pets Travel Scheme in the UK, visit www.defra.gov.uk/wildlife-pets/pets/travel/pets

CONDITIONS OF THE PET TRAVEL SCHEME

Different countries may have their own more specific requirements, but the following basic conditions must usually be met (in this exact order) –

- Dogs must have been microchipped first. This is to prevent mistaken identity and to ensure that the dog before officials is the dog listed in the pet passport.

- Dogs must have been given the rabies vaccine and then given a blood test to make sure they are free of rabies. This test is usually given 30 days after they get the rabies vaccine.

- Dogs must have been treated for ticks and tapeworms before they begin travel. This applies even if there is no sign that they have them. This treatment must happen between 24 hours and 48 hours before they travel. You need a signature from a vet on the pet passport to verify that it has been done. If you are traveling via the French port of Calais to the UK, you may need to get a French vet to do this treatment for you.

NOTE: Dogs that are under three months old cannot travel under the scheme as they are considered too young to get the rabies vaccine, which is essential for them to be granted a Pet Passport.

IS MICROCHIPPING SAFE?

As a condition of your dog traveling abroad, they must be microchipped. You may be worried about the side effects, but the truth is that microchipping is a very safe procedure that involves a chip the size of a grain of rice being put under the skin. This is a quick process.

From now on, your dog should be scanned whenever he goes to the vet's. This ensures the records they have are kept up to date.

Many dog charities recommend microchipping so that your dog will always find its way home to you. Most police stations and animal charities have scanners to check for microchipped pets.

TIP: Always make a note of the microchip number and take that with you when you travel.

For more information on microchips, see *page 31*.

TIP: After your dog has been microchipped, the vet will usually test it to make sure it works. If they don't test it, ask them to test it. It rarely happens, but chips can be faulty. If the chip stops working and you are traveling at the time, your poor pet may end up having to endure a six months stint in quarantine even when he has had all the vaccinations required for travel.

IS THE RABIES VACCINE SAFE?

Like all vaccinations, there are risks involved. But ask yourself this: is it worth the risk to prevent your dog getting a terrible disease and passing it onto others, maybe even humans?

There are other things to consider when talking about the rabies vaccine in connection with canine travel –

- Your dog may have to be vaccinated for rabies again, even if he already had the vaccine, if he was vaccinated before he was microchipped.

- Your vet should make a note of when the vaccine was administered and record the vaccine batch number, as well as your pet's details on the Pet Passport or vaccination certificate.

- If you believe your pet has suffered a reaction to the vaccination, contact your vet immediately. Ask them to look at your pet and to record the fact that they have had a reaction.

- Whether you plan to travel with your pet or not, the vet should still schedule a return visit for your dog so they can do a blood test to ensure the vaccine has worked. This should happen in around thirty days time.

- A booster vaccination should also be scheduled. To ensure Pet Passports are valid, vaccinations must be kept up to date.

TIP: Always check that the airline or ferry company you are using will carry dogs before you travel and ask them what their procedures are. In all cases, you will have to book travel for your dog before you go.

TRAVELING WITHIN THE USA

Due to the sheer size of America, taking your pet on vacation will almost certainly mean having to fly on a plane. See *What happens when my dog flies, page 102,* for more details.

There is one US internal airline that allows dogs to stay in the main cabin, in pet carriers. Fittingly called pet Airways, you can read about them more by visiting http://petairways.com. Destinations include New York, Baltimore and Los Angeles and your dog will even get their own flight attendant (they will have to share).

Check the website before you travel, as they are opening up new routes all the time.

Certain exclusions do apply to traveling with dogs in the USA – if you go to Hawaii, your dog will need to be in quarantine for 120 days (or 30 days if certain conditions are met).

TIP: If flying is too much for you and your dog, maybe a road trip would be best. Many animal charities, like the American Society for the Prevention of Cruelty to Animals (ASPCA), recommend that you only let your dog fly when its strictly necessary.

TRAVELING IN CANADA

If you use Air Canada's Jazz Flight, you can travel with your dog in the cabin with you, provided it is small enough to fit and stay comfortably in its carrier under the seat in front of you. You will need to make a reservation for your pet beforehand. If you don't, you will be turned away. Restrictions on routes do apply.

See www.aircanada.com/en/travelinfo/airport/baggage/pets.html for details.

NOTE: Pets are not allowed to travel in the cabin on flights to Hawaii from Canada. They are, however, allowed to sit in the cabin on flights from Hawaii.

Assistance dogs, such as guide dogs and hearing dogs, are also accommodated by Air Canada. They're allowed to sit at their owner's feet and are carried free of charge.

Their website also has details of government regulations concerning animals. Visit www.aircanada.com/en/travelinfo/airport/baggage/government-regulations.html for details.

NOTE: Dogs are not allowed on Canadian flights to or via the UK. They are only allowed on flights that originated from the UK, due to strict laws.

TRAVELING FROM THE USA & CANADA TO THE UK

The USA and Canada both qualify for the Pet Travel Scheme and have done so since 2002. The very specific conditions outlined under *Conditions of the Pet Travel Scheme* must be met.

Owners of pets from outside the European Community must tell Customs about their pet traveling with them. You may be have to pay a fee. If your dog is an assistance dog of any kind, if you notify them of this, they will try and reunite you with your dog as soon as possible.

Pets traveling on an approved sea route from the USA and guide dogs traveling on Eurostar need to be checked on arrival in the UK.

For pets traveling by air, the check will be carried out on arrival in the UK, by staff at the Animal Reception Center. If your dog fails the checks, he may be placed in quarantine.

NOTE: It's normal practice for the airline to cover flight and UK handling charges in their pet ticket price.

If your destination is the UK, there are certain types of dogs that will not be allowed into the country. This is because they are prohibited under The Dangerous Dog Act (1997).

The breeds are –

1. the Pit Bull Terrier (this is not a recognized breed in the UK, so the law is based on a dog having the characteristics of a pit bull, which has a stocky body and long, thick paws).

2. the Japanese tosa

3. the Dogo Argentino

4. the Fila Brasileiro

NOTE: The law changes all the time. Always check that your breed of dog isn't banned in the country you're going to before you travel.

TIP: If you are in doubt about your dog being one of those types of dog (whether they are is determined by how they look and, strangely, not breed), then ask your vet.

TRAVELING WITHIN EUROPE FROM THE UK

As well as meeting the criteria for the Pet Travel Scheme, dogs must wait at least 21 days from the date of their first rabies vaccine to travel within Europe from the UK. They must also not have been to any non-approved countries (these are ones with a high rabies risk) for at least six months before they leave or come back to the UK.

When traveling within Europe, going by ferry is the best way for you and your dog.

In many cases, your dog will be placed in a kennel on ferry services, note that there are some ferry services that allow your pet to remain in your car. Remember that you will need to produce your dog's pet passport at a reception center on the boat.

Dogs from the UK with Pet Passports can stay with their owners in their cars when they go on Brittany Ferries to certain destinations in Spain and France. See www.brittany-ferries.co.uk/pet-friendly-holidays/pets-travel-scheme for details.

You can also keep your dog in the car with you when traveling on DFDS Seaways Ferries, on various routes, including Denmark and Holland.

See www.dfdsseaways.co.uk/ferry-routes/pet-travel/pet-travel?gclid=CM-Slay-6KgCFQoa4Qods3KoCw for details. There's also a pet travel checklist.

Before you board the Euro tunnel shuttle service (this does not include the Eurostar) with your dog, you must take your pet to transport staff so that they can check the microchip and official documentation. Afterwards, you will be given a badge or sticker that must be displayed as instructed by the transport company staff and not be removed until you have left the port of arrival in the UK.

TIP: The only animals allowed on Eurostar, which is a train, are guide dogs.

TRAVELING TO NORTHERN IRELAND

There is one major difference to the rules that applies for the UK. All dogs coming into Northern Ireland from any approved country, including the USA and Canada, must have an Import License that has been previously issued by the Department of Agriculture and Rural Development. And, unless six months have passed since your pooch has had a rabies test, he will be placed in quarantine.

If six months have passed since the rabies blood test, your dog will still need to be taken to a quarantine station on arrival and checked out by a vet. Dogs that meet the criteria for entry will be handed back to their owners as soon as possible.

TIP: If traveling abroad, it may be a good idea to consider getting pet travel insurance. This works in a similar way to human travel insurance. You can buy it on a trip by trip basis, or get a full year's cover. Some pet insurance schemes covers traveling with your pet. See *Pet Travel Insurance, page 107,* for more information.

Check your policy or phone your insurer for clarification.

WHAT HAPPENS WHEN MY DOG FLIES?

For most dogs traveling from country to country will mean being placed in a pet carrier in the cargo hold of a plane. This can be a frightening prospect for any dog owner, thinking of their pet stuck in a cramped, dark space, but the good news is that it's not as bad as it sounds.

Airlines travel with pets all the time and will try and make sure your pet will be as comfortable as possible. The cargo hold is temperature controlled, so your dog will not be cold.

There are ways you can make your dog as comfortable as possible –

- Make sure the crate or pet carrier that he's in is secure (so he can't get out) and big enough for him to turn around in. The airline will advise you about this.

- Write your details on the outside of the crate so that there is no chance of him being misplaced. Include a note on whether you are on the same flight and what you and your dog's destination is.

- Make sure he has food and water. Remember, it is up to you to bring the dishes.

- Make him feel at home by putting his favorite toy or blanket in the crate. Familiar things will ease his anxiety.

- Print arrows on the crate to show the correct way up, so there will be no danger of him being lifted the wrong way up.

- Ask if someone will check on him during the flight. This may not always be possible, but there's no harm in asking.

- Don't be tempted to lock the crate. If your dog becomes ill, you want someone to be able to reach him quickly. And, there's a chance you could lose the key.

- Let staff know if your dog needs any medication during the flight. They might be able to help.

- Make sure the airline staff at your destination know your dog is onboard. They will be keen to get him off the plane as quickly as possible. Many of the staff will have dogs of their own and will understand why you are so anxious.

- Make sure you know where and when to collect him at the end of the flight. This avoids delays and you both getting anxious.

- If there is a delay with the flight, ask someone to check on your pet. Again, this may not be possible, but you won't know unless you ask, politely.

- Always aim for direct flights if possible. This means less stress for you and your dog.

- Tranquilizing your dog is generally not a good idea as this may hamper his breathing and you won't be there to notice. Ask your vet about gentler herbal remedies instead.

TIP: If your dog is going to be traveling in the cargo hold of a plane, its best to feed them long before you travel. It's also better for your dog, wherever possible, for you to travel at night as they may sleep through the entire journey, minimizing any stress for you and them.

TRAVELING WITH YOUR DOG ON A FERRY

There are some routes (mainly from the UK to other European Union countries, like Spain and France – see *Traveling within Europe from the UK*, page 101, where dogs can travel with you in your car. This is not always a good thing, especially on a hot day.

Wherever possible, never take your dog on a ferry on a hot day. Dogs should never be in hot cars.

Here are some tips to make the travel less stressful for your pet –

- If it's a long haul ferry, arrive early so you can put your car in the best place for your pet. Make sure your dog has been allowed out to do the toilet and get fresh air first before you embark.

- Make sure you know whether you need to report to a quarantine or reception station with your dog. This doesn't mean he will be taken away from you, just that his microchip with be scanned and his passport checked.

- Make sure your dog has fresh water whether he's in your car or has been placed on the ferry in a kennel.

- As long as it's not a very long trip, it might be a good idea not to feed him beforehand as he may be sick. If you must feed him, make it something light, like some turkey or chicken.

ESSENTIALS FOR CANINE TRAVEL

Packing for your dog should be like packing for yourself: do it with care and with all contingencies in mind.

- Remember to take any medication your dog is on, such as arthritis medication or insulin. Have a note of what this medication is in case you lose it and need to get more.

- Take a copy of your dog's Pet Passport. They will not be allowed to travel internationally without it as it details all of the vaccinations they have had, including that all important rabies one. In case you lose it or your luggage is misplaced, make a copy and put that in a different place.

- Take a note of your vet's name and phone number, in case you need to phone in an emergency or you need to take your pet to another vet, who may need to contact your vet.

- If your dog is a bad traveler, ask your vet for advice. They may give you valerian or some other medication to calm your dog down.

- Take a spare lead and collar – it can be easy to lose them, so pack a spare.

- Always take a water and food dish or a plastic dish that can be used in its place. If your dog is traveling with you, collapsible ones are best as they take up less space. If your dog is traveling in a crate (in the majority of cases, this is the only way he will be allowed to travel) normal dog dishes are best.

- Don't forget that all important favorite dog toy or favorite blanket.

- Make sure you are covered if your dog has an accident and needs emergency veterinary treatment. If you have it, carry a copy of your pet travel insurance policy or your pet insurance policy (if that covers travel. Check with the company before you leave that you are covered).

WILL MY PET INSURANCE INCLUDE TRAVEL INSURANCE?

Whereas ten years ago most dog owners had no pet insurance, these days having insurance is seen as the responsible thing to do. In the UK, there was even a move, which failed, to make it compulsory.

When you're abroad and your pet gets ill or injured, it can be a nightmare both emotionally and financially. That's why, for your own peace of mind, it may be a good idea to get pet insurance that covers your dog when they travel with you abroad.

You have two choices:

1. Pay for pet insurance that covers travel insurance in the policy. Note – this will make the money you pay each month more expensive and you will be paying for that additional cover whether you travel with your dog or not.

2. Get travel insurance for your dog that covers them for each trip or one that covers them for a period of time – usually a year.

In both cases, you will have to pay for some, or the entire vet's bill, and claim it back via the insurer. Check with your insurer.

PET TRAVEL INSURANCE

A typical pet travel policy will run along these lines –

- It will cover a single trip, a period of time such as a month, a year or even multiple trips during a full year.

- There will be a ceiling rate of cover. This should be enough to cover most eventualities. The cover starts from the day you leave until you get back home.

- Pet travel insurance can also cover the cost of quarantine fees (if needed), you having to cancel/shorten your holiday because your pet gets ill and repatriation fees if he goes missing.

- It may also cover the cost of you losing your pet's passport.

- Some breeds of dogs may be excluded from travel insurance, such as dog breeds known to have breathing problems, like Pugs. Certain breeds of dogs will cost more. This is because these breeds are prone to more problems and aren't known for their good health. This is standard with all types of pet insurance.

TIP: Like any insurance policy, keep an eye on what's not included in the policy as much as what is. And shop around for the best policy. But, remember, cost isn't everything. There's no point in paying for a policy that won't pay out when you need it. Like with any insurance, it's wise to go on personal recommendations.

WHAT TO DO IF YOUR DOG GETS LOST ABROAD

The good news is that this is unlikely to happen, but if the nightmare does happen, the procedure you follow is exactly the same as you would at home –

- Assuming your dog is microchipped, contact the microchip company immediately. They will inform you if anyone finds your dog.

- Tell everyone you meet that your dog is lost. Photocopy a picture if you can, or show people one you have on your camera or phone.

- Contact the local police or your embassy. Ask them for advice.

- Contact your pet insurer and let them know. They may be able to offer advice.

- Find out where any lost dogs that are picked up are taken. This varies from country to country. Some will go to dog pounds; others will be collected by wardens or the police.

- Use social networking sites like Twitter and Facebook. Change your avatar to a picture of your dog, say where you last saw him, what his name is and detail any distinguishing characteristics. Don't underestimate the power of the World Wide Web.

- List your dog on as many find a dog websites as you can. Put 'find lost dog' into a search engine and you will get a list. Ads should be free. Beware of sites that charge as they may not be genuine. See *Useful Websites, page 156,* for some sites aimed at reuniting people with their dogs.

- Make up posters and ask to place them in shop windows. Give your mobile phone number and make sure it is always turned on and fully charged. It may also be a good idea to offer a reward for anyone who finds your dog. It's sad, but true, that people are more likely to help you if there is a financial incentive.

PET FRIENDLY HOLIDAYS

You may not even have to travel out of the state or leave your country to take your pet on vacation. There are so many places to go where you can take your pet and are closer and won't involve a long flight.

For travel within the USA and Canada, go to www.dogfriendly.com. They have over 1000 dog friendly locations, as well as world-wide travel guides.

The site also lists parks where your dog can go off the leash, a parks and hiking guide for dogs and a guide to outdoor dining with your pet pooch.

For the UK, Channel Islands and the Isle of Man, visit www.takeyourpet. co.uk. They have a list of accommodation that does allow pets. They also have a section on traveling abroad (from the UK) with your dog.

TIP: In many cases, you will be charged an extra fee for your dog and the number of dogs you can take may be limited, often to two. You may also be asked for a deposit to cover any damage.

Old Age

" Old dogs, like old shoes, are comfortable. They might be a bit out of shape and a little worn around the edges, but they fit well. "

Bonnie Wilcox

Chapter 7
Old Age

Old age creeps up on everyone eventually, and, of course, our dogs are no exception to this. With their life crammed into a much shorter span than ours, their ageing process can sometimes feel very quick to us – one day he's a lively puppy and then, all of a sudden, he's got a grey muzzle and arthritic legs. But old age doesn't have to be all bad news for your dog, and here are some of my top tips for keeping that ageing dog looking – and feeling – in his prime!

WHAT AGE IS OLD FOR A DOG?

This is a tricky question, as different dogs tend to age at different rates. But there is a way to get a rough idea of your dog's human age.

The first thing to say is that the well-known formula of one dog year being equal to seven human years is no use at all. The best way to work out your dog's human age is by following one of these formulae:

- For little dogs (up to 10kg) – 12 human years per dog year for the first two years, and then 4 per year thereafter. So a 10 year old terrier will be 56 and a 15 year old will be 76.

- For medium dogs (10-30kg) – 10 human years per dog year for the first two years, and then 5 per year thereafter. A 10 year old spaniel, for example, will be 60 and a 15 year old will be 85.

- For big dogs (30kg +) – A bit simpler – 8 human years per dog year all the way. So an 8 year old German Shepherd will be roughly 64 in human terms.

CARING FOR AN OLDER DOG

A NEW BED

However old your ageing dog is in human terms, there's no doubt she'll appreciate a comfy bed, as older dogs are often prone to aches and pains, especially when the weather is cold and wet. So to make sure your ageing dog is as comfortable as possible, think about upgrading her bed and positioning it somewhere that is totally draft-free and nice and cosy. You can buy a top quality pet bed from your local pet shop, or, if you want to save a little money, why not try a little lateral thinking?

One clever idea is to buy a cheap 'egg-crate' foam mattress, cut it in half and place one half on top of the other to give a thick, smooth mattress, which you can then cover in a washable fabric. Or for a really big dog, why not drag that old inflatable camping mattress out of the garage and cover it in a thick blanket – as long as she doesn't chew a hole in it, it will make a super soft bed for her!

As your dog gets older, he'll probably get a bit slower and less keen to go racing off after squirrels and rabbits. This doesn't mean that he's not enjoying his walks though – just that he's taking life at a slightly slower pace. The best way to keep an older dog fit and happy is to make sure he gets plenty of regular walks, but keep them fairly short and try to make sure he doesn't overdo it. Keep ball throwing and stick chasing to a minimum as this puts a lot of stress on the joints and heart, and concentrate on quiet rambles in the countryside or park.

TEACH AN OLD DOG NEW TRICKS!

Here's a great way to rekindle the spark of life in your old dog – take her to a training class and teach her some new tricks. Don't go for anything too adventurous; just try to teach her some interesting new tricks or commands, such as rolling onto her back, or covering her eyes with her paws. Use healthy treats to encourage her when she gets the new trick right, and you'll soon find that this new focus has put a puppy-like spring back into her step!

DIET FOR OLDER DOGS

When you're looking after an elderly dog, it's even more important to get their diet spot on than when they were younger. Older animals can't tolerate high levels of proteins or fats and need to eat a diet that meets their specific nutritional needs. They generally need less energy, and a bit more fiber, and although they need a reasonable amount of protein to keep them in shape, too much will put a strain on their kidneys. Ideally, you should feed a diet based on proteins, like chicken and fish, which can be used most efficiently, and avoid foods with beef and other red meat proteins.

The best way of making sure your older dog is getting just the right mix of nutrients he needs is to feed him a top quality dried complete food. Choose one without artificial additives like preservatives and flavorings, and aim for a protein level of around 18-24% (adult dog foods usually have about 22-28% protein).

However, just because your dog is getting on a bit, it doesn't mean you have to stop cooking him the occasional home-cooked meal – far from it. Giving him a healthy treat with one of these recipes is a great way of topping up his reservoirs of vitamins and nutrients, and they're all specially formulated so as not to put a strain on the kidneys. They've also got some stronger flavors, as older dogs don't smell as well as they used to (in more ways than one in some cases…)

WHITE FISH AND RICE

Dog food doesn't get much healthier than this, and the added coriander will help tickle the older dog's taste buds. It's got a moderate level of protein, which is all highly digestible, meaning less work for the kidneys.

To feed a couple of hungry hounds, you will need:

- 250g white fish fillet

- 300ml milk

- 1 teaspoon fresh lemon juice

- 1 teaspoon olive oil

- 1 tablespoon fresh coriander

- 125g brown rice

Put the rice on to cook as brown rice takes a good half an hour. Then cover the fish with the milk, bring to the boil and then remove from the heat, allowing the fish to cook in hot milk for about 5 minutes.

Then remove the fish from the milk and crumble it into a dish with the lemon juice and oil. Mix in the cooked and drained rice and finally add the chopped up coriander.

CHICKEN, SPINACH AND SARDINE MASH

The combination of the easy-to-digest protein from the chicken, with the good quality carbohydrate from the sweet potato, and the vitamins from the spinach makes this recipe super healthy – and the sardines add in essential omega-3 oils as well as a bit of extra taste.

You need:

- 250g chicken mince

- 400g sweet potatoes

- 250g spinach, shredded

- 1 tin sardines in oil

- ½ teaspoon egg shell powder (*see the Fishy Delight recipe, page 74*) or 1x1000mg calcium supplement, crushed.

- 1 teaspoon brewer's yeast (if available)

Boil the sweet potatoes in their skins until tender (about ten minutes), and then drain and mash them. At the same time, gently fry the chicken mince without adding any fat, until it is cooked through, then add the spinach and cook for a few minutes until it is reduced down.

Finally, add the sardines, along with all the oil, to the mince and spinach, and mix it all together with the mash in a mixing bowl. Add in the calcium or egg shell, and the brewer's yeast and form into egg-sized balls.

OLD DOG POWER JUICE

There's no doubt that fresh fruit and veg help to keep old age at bay – lots of studies have proven that eating plenty of fruit and veg reduces the risk of all sorts of diseases, including cancer. Getting a dog, especially an old boy, to eat down a plate of fruit and veg is nigh on impossible – which is why I've come up with this cunning recipe for a revitalizing juice drink old dogs will love. Feed him this once a week and you'll keep him fighting fit for years to come!

- 100g chicken liver
- 300g assorted fruit and veg – anything you have to hand (except onions, tomatoes and mushrooms)

Put the liver in a small bowl and pour over just enough boiling water to cover it. Let it stand for ten minutes.

Meanwhile, chuck all the veg and fruit into the blender. Anything goes here – apples, plums, cabbage, zucchinis, carrots – as long as it's fruit or veg and it's not an onion, tomato or mushroom, in it goes. Whiz it all up to make a thick puree. Then add in the liver, complete with its water.

Blend together, adding more water if necessary, until you have a thick drink. Pour a reasonable amount into the dog bowl and watch her slurp it up. You can freeze the rest if you have some left over.

BLOOD TESTS

As your dog gets older, he might continue to look fit and healthy on the outside, but this isn't always the whole story. Internally, things can be

" If a dog will not come to you after having looked you in the face, you should go home and examine your conscience. "

Woodrow Wilson

starting to go wrong, and, if left unchecked, these underlying problems can suddenly turn into full-blown, life-threatening illnesses. In order to combat these internal problems, which can include kidney disease, liver disease, cancer and diabetes, you need to find them before they become obvious, by which time it's often too late. When your dog reaches middle age (perhaps 50 in human terms), ask your vet for a general blood test. This will check all your dog's internal systems and will either give him a clean bill of health or will enable you to tackle any problems that exist. Repeat these tests every few years as he enters old age to make sure nothing is missed.

In the worst cases of arthritis, and in some other conditions affecting the legs, dogs can end up so crippled they can't even walk. However, this doesn't necessarily have to be the end, as there is a solution that can work wonders, especially if it's only the back legs that are affected.

What you need to do is fit your dog with a set of wheels! Now this might sound crazy, but there are several companies out there who make special harnesses for dogs, which support their back end above two wheels. The front legs then simply pull the weak back end around, and the dog carries on as if there's no problem at all!

DEAFNESS

Deafness is another common problem for older dogs, but it rarely causes serious problems – apart from that selective type of deafness, which enables dogs to ignore commands out in the park but hear the slightest sound of a tin of dog food being opened from a hundred yards away!

If your dog is starting to lose his hearing, there are a few important tips that will help him – and you – cope with the problem.

- Use sign language as much as possible when giving commands. Get him used to responding to visual signals rather than just verbal commands.

- Thump the floor with your foot to get his attention through the vibrations in the ground.

COMMON HEALTH PROBLEMS IN OLDER DOGS

ARTHRITIS

Arthritis is one of the most common problems for older dogs, causing pain and immobility in a high proportion of elderly dogs. There are many causes, ranging from badly formed joints (such as hip dysplasia) to simple wear and tear, but whatever the original cause of the problem, there's a lot you can do to help. Here are my top tips for looking after an arthritic dog:

1. Early diagnosis is vital, so look out for the first signs of arthritis, which include stiffness after exercise, reluctance to jump or climb stairs, lameness in one or more legs and general lethargy and depression.

2. Regular short walks are much better than less frequent, long periods of exercise.

3. Weight is crucial as every extra pound on your dog's waistline puts extra pressure on the painful joints, so try to get that extra weight off with a lower calorie diet.

4. Your vet can prescribe anti-inflammatory drugs that help to reduce swelling and pain.

5. Food supplements and tablets, which contain glucosamine and chondritin sulphate (from your vet), help the joints repair themselves and reduce pain.

6. A teaspoon of cod liver oil every day provides a great source of omega 3 fatty acids and vitamin D, both of which help keep joints and bones healthy.

- Don't surprise him! Make sure you approach him from where he can see you, so as not to give him too much of a shock when you touch him.

- Keep him on a lead. If he can't hear you, and goes too far away to see your visual commands, he could easily get lost, so it's best to keep him on a long lead in the park.

- Accept that his hearing will inexplicably improve whenever there's food about!

DID YOU KNOW?

Sharp hearing is important for all dogs, domestic or wild. Dogs are able to hear sounds that we cannot. Their super-sensitive ears respond both to lower volumes and higher pitched sounds.

Have you ever seen a dog prick up its ears? Dog ears are more mobile than ours are, and a dog can adjust them to maximize reception. Eighteen or more muscles tilt, raise and rotate a dog's ears for the best possible sound reception.

The shape of a dog's ears helps with hearing, too. Just as we cup our hands around our ears so we can hear better, a dog's upright, curved ears help direct and amplify sound. Erect ears, like those of wild dogs, hear better than the floppy ears of many domestic breeds.

Dogs hear higher frequency sounds than humans although not quite as high as cats can. Frequency, the number of sound wave cycles every second, is measured in a unit called Hertz (Hz). The higher the frequency, the more sound waves per second, the higher pitched the sound.

Foxes, jackals and other wild canines can't always get a glimpse of their prey. Instead, they might use their ears to find it. For a fox, a rustle of grass or a tiny squeak is an invitation to dinner.

Dogs' excellent hearing was probably one of the first reasons we tolerated wolves and early dogs near our camps. For centuries, we have used them

as sentries and guards, alerting us to possible danger. This is especially important at night, when it's hard for us to see.

DID YOU KNOW?

At the end of the Beatles' song "A Day in the Life", an ultrasonic whistle, audible only to dogs, was recorded by Paul McCartney for his Shetland sheepdog.

CATARACTS

Along with hearing problems, many old dogs also suffer from problems with their eyes. The most common cause of poor vision and blindness is cataracts, which are opaque areas in the lens of the eye, and can be caused by diabetes, or just by old age. Nowadays, cataracts can be removed using an ultrasound probe, which dissolves the lens and removes it from the eye, but this isn't suitable for all dogs, and some are just too old to go through a procedure like this. So what else can you do to help your dog if she is losing her sight? Well here are two easy tips that should make her life a lot easier…

1. Don't move the furniture – dogs get to know where everything is in the house and can navigate around even if their sight is poor. If you move things around, they will be confused and bump into things!

2. Dab a dilute vinegar solution onto sharp corners and new items – this will help her smell the obstacle before she walks into it!

DID YOU KNOW?

Dogs don't see the same way humans do. They have a wider field of view and a better ability to detect motion on the horizon. A dog can recognize moving objects nearly half a mile (1 km) away. But if those objects remain still, the dog may not notice them. This is very helpful in hunting fast moving prey.

Dogs don't see color very well because they don't have as many color-sensitive cells (cones) in their eyes. They can, however, see much better in the dark than we can, as a dog's eyes have more dim light receptors called rods.

There's another reason why dogs see much better at night than humans. Like many other mammals, the dog has a mirror-like tissue in its eyes. This tissue enhances night vision by reflecting incoming light back through the retina. This re-stimulates the eyes' light-sensing cells and boosts their signal to the brain. If your torch catches Fido's eyes at night, you'll see this reflected light gleaming back at you as 'eyeshine'.

Humans and dogs have been hunting together for thousands of years. Most canines (wild and domestic) rely on all of their senses to be successful hunters. However, there are certain types of dogs, called 'gaze' or 'sight hounds', which have been bred to rely more on their sight than hearing or smell. Some of the oldest breeds, these animals carefully scan the horizon for motion. Once the prey is spotted, they rely on their amazing speed to chase the prey down. Whippets, greyhounds, and salukis are just a few examples of sight hounds.

DID YOU KNOW?

1. Longevity in domestic dogs depends on the care they receive, their breed, and body size.

2. In general, larger breeds have shorter lifespans.

3. Many giant dog breeds average only 7 or 8 years, while some small terrier breeds might live as long as 20 years.

4. The average lifespan for mixed-breed and midsize dogs is about 13 to 14 years. The longest-lived dog with reliable documentation died at 29 in 1939.

Emergencies

" A good dog never dies. He always stays. He walks beside you on crisp autumn days when frost is on the fields and winter's drawing near. His head is within our hand in his old way. "

Mary Carolyn Davies

Chapter 8
Emergencies

Knowing what to do in case of an emergency or accident involving your dog is a really good idea – and could even save your dog's life.

COMMON EMERGENCIES:

CUTS

One of the most common emergency situations faced by dog owners is the cut pad or paw. A sharp piece of glass or metal in the undergrowth can easily cause a deep and nasty cut, and when dog's paws are cut, they tend to bleed an awful lot!

In a situation like this, you have got two main priorities. Firstly you need to try and stop the bleeding as much as you can – and this is where socks come in – and secondly you need to get to your vet a.s.a.p.

To get the bleeding under control, take off both of your socks. Pull one over the bleeding paw, and then use the other to tie the first sock securely in place. If possible, pass the second sock around the area where the cut is so that it applies firm direct pressure to the wound. Then give your vet a ring to let them know you are on your way, and get straight down there without delay.

Finally, it is worth mentioning that although a bleeding pad can look very alarming and distressing, a little blood goes a very long way, and even though your dog might appear to be losing a lot of blood, in reality it is very unlikely to be life-threatening. So try to keep yourself and your dog as calm as possible. In the vast majority of cases, after a proper bandage or stitches at the vets, the outcome will be fine.

7 FIRST AID ESSENTIALS

1. Know your vet's emergency number so you can call for advice any time of day or night – best to keep it in your cell (mobile) phone.

2. Find out where you will need to take your pet in an emergency out of normal working hours – many vets are covered by different practices at night and you need to know how to get there in an emergency.

3. Keep a basic first aid kit at home and in the car, with bandages and antiseptic cream.

4. Always have a supply of fresh water available when you're out and about, especially in hot weather when it can be a life-saver for an over-heating dog.

5. Keep a thick blanket in the car to wrap up your pet if they are injured. This will help keep them warm and, if he's a large dog, help you carry him to and from the car easily and without doing further damage to any injuries.

6. Research any problems that particularly affect your breed of dog – for example, big dogs like Wolfhounds and Great Danes are prone to bloat and to twisted stomachs and it's important that you know what to look for.

7. Take out good pet insurance so that money never becomes an obstacle to treatment.

STINGS AND BITES

In the summer, lots of dogs end up with bee stings, especially around the mouth after they chase and try to swallow a bee. The resulting sting can be very painful and cause a big swelling of the lips and face.

However, a simple sting doesn't have to turn into a crisis. If you know that a bee was to blame (either you saw the bee, or you can spot the sting embedded in the dog's mouth) then head to the kitchen and find some bicarbonate of soda. Rub a small amount over the swollen area, and this will reduce the acidity of the sting and help to bring down the swelling.

Unlike bees, which have an acidic sting, wasp's stings are alkaline, so to neutralize them, dab some vinegar over the swollen area. You can tell that a sting was caused by a wasp and not a bee because wasps don't leave their sting behind.

Snake bites are uncommon in dogs, but do occur. Symptoms of a bite usually include a rapid and painful swelling localized around two small puncture marks, and more serious complications are very uncommon. The best course of action is to keep the dog as quiet as possible and take him to your vet as quickly as possible, where a strong anti-inflammatory injection will usually sort out the problem.

In countries where more venomous snakes exist, it is important to immobilize the bite site to prevent the toxin spreading, especially if it is on a limb, and get veterinary assistance as soon as possible.

DOGFIGHTS

You're walking your dog on a lead in the park, minding your own business, when all of a sudden, in a flash of black and tan, another dog races up and launches its teeth into your dog's neck. You panic, and try desperately to pull the attacker off but to no avail.

Situations like this are not uncommon and can be very distressing for dog and owner alike. But what can you do to help? Well here are a few important dos and don'ts for breaking up a dog fight:

- Screaming and shouting won't help!

- Never get anywhere near the biting end of either dog – in the heat of battle, even your own dog might inadvertently bite you.

- The best technique is to grab the dogs by their back legs, lift them up like a wheelbarrow, and pull them apart.

- If you are on your own, loop a lead around the back legs of one dog and tie it to a solid object, like a tree or fence. Then move around to the second dog, and pull him away by the back legs.

- Make sure you secure both dogs before letting go of the legs – otherwise they'll be straight back at each other.

ROAD TRAFFIC ACCIDENTS

Cars are one of the biggest killers of dogs. Every day, dogs are killed and injured as they run out in front of cars and are knocked down. Of course, the best thing is to prevent your dog from being at risk. Make sure she's always on the lead whenever you're near a busy road, no matter how well behaved you think she is; and check the security of your garden to make sure she can never escape and end up wandering onto a road.

If the worst does happen though, there are a few important things to remember, which could help save your dog's life.

Firstly, make sure she is safe from further injury. If she's lying in the road, carry her gently to the verge and make her comfortable there.

Secondly, identify and stop any obvious bleeding by applying direct pressure through a rolled up t-shirt or other item of clothing.

And finally, get her to your own vet straight away (or emergency vet if it is out of hours), as they will be able to assess her injuries and get her treated straight away.

STICK INJURIES

You throw a stick for the dog and when he comes back there's something wrong – he can't close his mouth properly and he's constantly pawing at his face in obvious distress. Has he been bitten or stung? Or even run into a tree in his excitement?

The answer is almost certainly not – and the solution to his problem can be easily found if you take a look inside his mouth. What you'll probably find is a piece of stick wedged between his teeth at the top of his mouth. This is quite a common problem, caused when an over-enthusiastic dog races onto a stick and it breaks off in his mouth.

The solution requires a bit of lateral thinking… and a toolkit! Dig out a pair of pliers from the car or garage, and grab hold of the offending stick. Then twist the stick sideways to loosen it from the teeth, and hey presto, it should pop out without too much difficulty!

HEATSTROKE

Heatstroke is a major danger to dogs and results in many deaths every year, often in tragic circumstances, such as dogs being left in parked cars. The reason that dogs are so prone to this problem is down to the way they regulate their temperature. Rather than relying on sweat to evaporate, like we do, dogs rely on panting to discharge heat from their tongues.

An overheated dog breathes in and out through its mouth. With each pant, dogs inhale cool air. As the cool air moves into the lungs, it absorbs heat and moisture. When dogs exhale hot breath across a wet tongue, water evaporates, cooling their bodies. To maximize heat loss, panting dogs direct warm blood to their tongue to be cooled. The hot, moist air the dog exhales is some 10°F warmer than if it exited through the nose, helping to rapidly dump body heat. But just like sweating, panting cools by evaporation and a panting dog needs access to plenty of drinking water.

This works very well provided there is a plentiful supply of cool fresh air – but in enclosed situations where the air quickly becomes saturated with moisture and very warm, their body temperature can rapidly rise with devastating results. It can often take only a matter of minutes for a dog to become dangerously overheated and die, even in situations where the weather may not be obviously hot. The simple rule to prevent this ever happening to your dog is to never, ever leave your dog in a car, even on cool days, and always make sure they have access to fresh water and fresh air.

DIARRHEA

Diarrhea is a really common problem in dogs, and it can be caused by lots of things, including bacterial infections, bowel inflammation and food allergies. Here are my tips for dealing with this unpleasant problem!

1. If there's a mess in the house, clean it up well using a strong disinfectant. Make sure you wash your hands well afterwards and keep children away from the scene of the crime!

2. No food. In mild cases, a 12 hour fast should do the trick, but generally 24 hours is best.

3. Plenty of water. Don't ever withhold water as dehydration is the real worry with diarrhea.

4. Make an electrolyte replacement solution. If the diarrhea continues for more than a few days, make up a pint of warm water with a teaspoon of salt and a tablespoon of sugar mixed in. Offer this instead of water as it will help replace all the essential electrolytes being lost in the diarrhea.

5. Boiled chicken and rice. When you reintroduce food after starving him, cook up something really easy to digest, like chicken breast and brown rice. Gradually change back to his old food over the next few days if all is well.

6. Yoghurt. Give natural live yoghurt once he's starting to eat again. The probiotics produced by the yoghurt bacteria can help your dog's intestines recover more quickly.

7. If in doubt – go to the vet. Diarrhea can be a really serious problem, especially in old or very young dogs, so err on the side of caution and get a veterinary opinion if things aren't getting better.

VOMITING

Being sick can be a sign of serious ill health – but it can also be perfectly normal for lots of dogs. I've known many dogs who would regularly bring back their dinner every now and then (and then proceed to wolf it down again of course!) so you shouldn't worry if your dog develops a similar habit. It's generally caused by over-eating or eating too quickly, and if you want to stop it, try feeding smaller meals more frequently.

On the other hand, though, persistent vomiting can be a sign of serious problems, and if your dog suddenly starts being sick it's important to get to the vet for a checkup as soon as possible.

One of the most serious and quickly life-threatening canine emergencies is bloat caused by a twisted stomach. This is mainly a problem for big dogs like German Shepherds and Great Danes, and it tends to occur after they've eaten a big meal and then had some vigorous exercise. What happens is the stomach twists around and then becomes massively bloated with gas. If not treated very quickly, this can lead to fatal complications, so it's really important to recognize the signs and get veterinary help as soon as possible if you suspect this condition. The main things to look out for are:

" For me a house or an apartment becomes a home when you add one set of four legs, a happy tail, and that indescribable measure of love that we call a dog. "

Roger Caras

- Hard, bloated stomach

- Vomiting and retching up white froth

- Pain and discomfort

The best tips for preventing the problem occurring in the first place are to feed at least twice a day, rather than in one big meal, and to avoid any exercise within two hours of a meal.

ALTERNATIVE REMEDIES

Not all doggy disasters are real emergencies. Sometimes it's just a case of stress that's causing problems, and, in these cases, there's nothing better than a few drops of good old Rescue Remedy.

Rescue Remedy is a mix of five herbs, which was first formulated 70 years ago by a Dr Bach as a treatment for stress in people. Nowadays, its well documented effects have been shown to work for dogs as well as people, and so it's well worth having on standby if you're about to move house, or there's another stressful situation coming up.

To use it, just pop a couple of drops on your dog's tongue or in her water and she should be relaxed and stress free for several hours.

ALOE VERA FOR STINGS, CUTS AND GRAZES

Most people know Aloe Vera for its skin soothing properties in people – it can be found in lots of skin products, and there is real scientific evidence to back up the claims that it actually can help skin healing. So why not use it on your dog as well? Aloe Vera gel or cream is great for grazes, cuts and stings because it promotes rapid healing and soothes the pain of damaged skin.

Joe's Canine Casebook

" No one appreciates the very special genius of your conversation as the dog does. "

Christopher Morley

Chapter 9
Joe's Canine Casebook

Over the 15 years I've been a practicing vet, I've kept a diary of interesting cases I've seen. These have involved patients of all shapes and sizes, from tiny hamsters right up to cattle and horses, with all sorts of problems, from the everyday to the unusual. There are probably more dogs in my casebook than any other species, and here are a few of the more memorable canine cases I've seen down the years:

A PROBLEM SHARED...

Arthritis is one of the most common ailments affecting my patients, but, until recently, I'd never personally experienced the pain of joint problems myself. Over the last couple of months, however, I've had a really sore shoulder, and the way this has affected me, and the response I've found with various treatments, has really opened my eyes to how our pets suffer from and cope with arthritic pain.

The term arthritis literally means 'inflamed joint' and can be used to cover a wide range of diseases, including joint infections (septic arthritis), auto-immune arthritis (rheumatism) and the most common form, osteoarthritis, or inflammation related to the bones of the joints.

Osteoarthritis is commonly caused by instability in joints or badly formed joints – and the two classic forms of the disease in dogs are arthritis related to knee ligament damage causing an unstable joint, and the hereditary condition of hip dysplasia where a badly formed joint causes arthritis. All vets see these kind of cases every day, and treating them makes up a significant proportion of our everyday work. And it's not just us vets who are dealing with arthritic joints – as my doctor said to me when I took my sore shoulder in last week, stiff and sore joints also make up a large amount of his caseload as well.

The diagnosis in my case was a strained shoulder rather than osteoarthritis, which was a relief as it should clear up completely, given rest and time. However, the pain and discomfort I have experienced with even this mild case of joint pain has certainly made me empathize more with my patients suffering with their joints.

The day after I'd been to the doctor about my shoulder, I saw a very typical case of osteoarthritis in a very typical breed – the Golden retriever. These large dogs are one of the more commonly affected breeds, due to their size and tendency to have hip problems, including dysplasia, and this case was classic of the early stage arthritis cases I see.

The dog is 6 years old and has been getting stiff in his back legs for several months now. According to his owners, he used to jump in and out of the car with no problems, but now he is much more reluctant and needs to be helped up. He's also very stiff in the evenings, especially after a long walk in the day, and has started to get a bit grumpy, which is very out of character.

After an examination where I could feel the grating of arthritic joints in his back legs, it was clear that he was suffering from osteoarthritis as a result of badly formed joints, especially in his hips. Unfortunately, it was too late to consider any treatments to prevent the onset of the disease, but there are many very effective treatments that can help in these cases, including pain-killing anti-inflammatory medications, one of which I prescribed in this instance.

As well as the pain killer, I have also started this dog on a course of glucosamine, which is a dietary supplement that has been proven to help reduce the symptoms of arthritis, and advised his owners to limit his exercise to several short walks rather than long strenuous hikes, and also put him on a strict diet to get his weight down.

With all of these measures in place I am confident that he will improve, although the long term outlook is less positive due to his relatively young age. If he does deteriorate, there is a chance that we will have to consider some more radical options, including hip replacement surgery.

And as for my shoulder – once I stop all this typing and get back to the surgery, I think it will be fine!

BIG TROUBLE!

Owning a badly behaved dog can be trouble – but owning a big badly behaved dog can be more than just trouble, it can be disastrous. Milo the St Bernard is a classic example of when big dogs go wrong and cause their owners all sorts of problems.

I first met Milo about a year ago when he was just 4 months old. His owners, the Evans family, had just brought him home from a breeder and he needed his first vaccination.

'Why did you not get him until now?' I asked as I examined Milo, who was already the size of a large Labrador, even at this young age, 'most people take puppies at two or three months.'

'Oh it was the breeder,' said Mrs Evans, 'she said she didn't want to let him go to a new home until he was this age.'

This worried me immediately, as the family had already missed out on the prime period for socialising with a dog, between three and four months of age. After this time, the dog is much less susceptible to new ideas and training, and it can be much harder to bring up the dog properly starting so late.

But what happened next made me far more worried than Milo's late start in his family life. I went to look in his mouth, to check his teeth, and, without warning, he suddenly let out a mean growl and snapped his teeth aggressively – narrowly missing my hand.

'Milo!' said Mr Evans, as I retreated, checking my hand for missing fingers.

'He's always doing that,' announced one of the children proudly.

'Hmm, well you're going to have to teach him not to,' I ordered sternly, 'otherwise he's going to be a real handful when he's fully grown.'

Over the next year, things went from bad to worse, as Milo began to take over the Evans family home. What started off as the occasional nip and growl, quickly turned into complete dominance, and, within six months, no-one except Mr Evans had any hope of controlling the enormous dog.

Things came to head a few weeks ago when Mrs Evans rang up in floods of tears.

'It's Milo, he's bitten Daisy.'

Thankfully, it turned out that the bite wasn't serious, but things couldn't go on like this. Next time, her daughter might not be so lucky, and I couldn't let them carry on putting their children's safety at risk.

'I think you've got two real options,' I told the gathered family later that day, 'either we look for a new home for Milo, or he goes off to see a behavior specialist to see what can be done for him.'

To my surprise, considering what had just happened, the family opted to take Milo to Oxford and see a behavioral specialist. I wasn't overly hopeful, considering the extent of Milo's problems, and so I was very surprised that the next time I saw the dog he was a model of good behavior, and the family were ecstatic with the changes the therapy had brought about.

'He's a totally different dog!' said Mrs Evans, proudly stroking Milo's head.

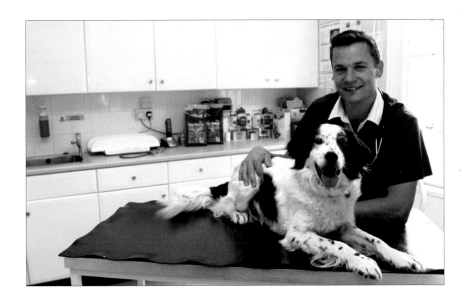

'I'm amazed, I must admit,' I said as I examined Milo. There wasn't a hint of aggression from him during the entire consultation.

'We're so pleased,' said Mr Evans, 'the therapy has made such a difference to him – and to us at home.'

Changes like this are rare, but they can happen, and it just goes to show that you can do something about a badly behaved dog – even a big badly behaved dog!

GREED!

There's a saying that goes 'too much of a good thing can be bad for you' and I've seen a case this week that illustrates this point. It involved a four month old Labrador puppy called Alfie and a large bag of dried dog food. According to the worried lady on the end of the phone, Alfie had broken into the kitchen while she had been out and gorged himself on the dog food, leaving just a few scraps of packaging and the odd stray kibble on the floor. By the time she got home, Alfie was fast asleep amidst the remains of his feast. Initially, Alfie's owner wasn't too worried, after all it was the food he ate every day, so surely it wouldn't be too bad for him, she thought. However, within a few hours, it was clear that all was not well. Alfie had looked a little rounder than usual when she'd first found him, but his stomach seemed to be swelling and swelling as time went by, and by the time she reached for the phone to ring the surgery, his belly was painfully distended and he was in some obvious discomfort.

Morning surgery had just finished when she rang, and I was about to start operating, but, after hearing Alfie's symptoms, I told her to come straight down – it sounded as if Alfie might have a serious problem, which could even be life-threatening if left alone for too long.

A Volvo estate pulled into the car park ten minutes later, and a mother and tribe of anxious-looking children rushed through to the consulting room with a bemused and very fat chocolate brown puppy in their arms.

'This is Alfie' announced one of the children ' and he's eaten all of his food!'

It looked as if Alfie had eaten a whole shop-full of dog food, rather than just a bag – his stomach was twice as big as normal, and solid to the touch. He was slightly uncomfortable, but still managed a friendly lick as I examined him, and, amazingly, was greedily eying up the pile of dog food bags in the corner of the room.

'He'll eat anything' said the lady 'It's a nightmare sometimes, trying to keep an eye on him the whole time.'

'He once tried to eat my teddy bear!' said the smallest child, patting Alfie affectionately.

'Well, he's certainly eaten himself into a bit of trouble this time.' I said 'If we don't do something, there's a risk his stomach might twist, which would be very serious, or that all the food inside will keep on swelling up and damage his stomach.'

The first thing to do was to try and make Alfie be sick, to get rid of some of the food in his stomach. If that didn't work, and he continued to swell up, an operation to remove the food would be the only option left.

Dogs are often sick at inopportune moments, and in the least appropriate places, but trying to make a dog be sick when you want it to is another matter. We tried mustard, salty water, washing soda, and a few other old-wives tricks, but nothing seemed to be working. Alfie gulped a few times, but otherwise seemed to be quite enjoying all the attention. Then, just as I was resigning myself to a big and tricky operation, Alfie wandered over to the edge of the car park, nibbled a little grass, and then, with an almighty heave, up came an enormous pile of half-digested dog food. After a few minutes, Alfie was back to his normal size, and everyone was breathing huge sighs of relief. Alfie seemd entirely oblivious to all the fuss, and wandered over to the food stand and stared at the bags with hungry eyes.

'He hasn't learnt his lesson.' I said, watching Alfie licking his lips.

'No, but I have' replied his owner 'from now on all his food is going to be locked away!'

THE CASE OF THE MISSING RUBBER TOY...

There are some cases in a vet's life that seem to happen once a year, every year – the cat trapped in the car engine compartment, the dog with a stick jammed in his mouth and so on. These cases are unusual, but seem to happen on a regular basis (if that makes any sense). As a newly qualified vet, you are amazed the first time you see one of these cases, but then after seeing one or two every year, it becomes less of a surprise and more of a case of 'Oh no, here we go again!'

Last week I saw my seemingly annual case involving a dog and a missing rubber toy. I think I've seen a case like this pretty much every year since I qualified back in 1996, and despite that fact, I am always surprised by what I end up removing from inside a dog's intestines. One year it was an entire bouncing ball, another it was half a rubber bone – and this year the missing rubber object was a large round toy that the patient in question, a 4 year old collie called Sam, had devoured over the course of a weekend.

'He's a real devil for chewing his toys,' explained Sam's owner apologetically, 'I'm always having to grab things from him. He nearly swallowed an entire tennis ball last year!'

This time though it seemed as though Sam had been a little too quick for her and half of the toy was unaccounted for and presumed swallowed.

'Every time he eats, it's just coming straight back up,' said Sam's owner as I palpated his abdomen, 'and he's getting really miserable.'

'I can feel something inside,' I replied, 'and it is probably the missing toy I'm afraid, in which case he'll almost certainly need an operation to remove it.'

An x-ray quickly confirmed that the lump in Sam's abdomen was indeed the missing toy, a situation that left us little choice but to operate and remove it surgically. If left inside, there was a slim chance that it would work its way through and out the other end, but, more probably, it would remain stuck in place and cause potentially life-threatening complications.

The surgery required to remove a 'foreign body' such as this is generally fairly straight forward – and very rewarding. It is one of those instances when you know that the operation will completely cure the patient if it goes well. In Sam's case, the remains of the toy were lodged in his small intestine and the operation to remove it went very well.

Sam will make a good recovery, and hopefully this will teach him a lesson about not swallowing things he shouldn't – otherwise he could be back next year for my 'missing rubber toy hunt'! In the meantime, it must be around the time when my next 'cat stuck in car engine compartment' case comes in… if only our pets would learn their lessons!

OLD AGE CATCHES UP WITH US ALL

Just like ourselves, as pets get older, they become prone to more and more diseases and problems – in simple terms, the body starts to fail bit by bit over time as the wear and tear of everyday life takes its toll, and this leads to illness and health problems. The most serious example of this is the incidence of cancer in older animals, with nearly all types of malignant growth becoming more common as pets get older, but there are many other diseases that occur more frequently as pets age, including arthritis, heart disease and many others.

Part of the reason we see so many health problems in older pets is simply because our pets live longer lives nowadays. A few decades ago, when pets lived on household scraps and vets had only the most basic treatments available, it was unusual for cats and dogs to live into their mid-teens or beyond, but today, with modern healthy diets and state of the art medical and surgical facilities, more and more pets are living longer. And with this aging population of pets comes a whole range of diseases and health problems that were unusual years ago but are becoming commonplace nowadays.

Take Peppy, a dog I saw recently, for example. At 15 years of age she's well into her old age, and is really living well beyond what could be termed a natural lifespan for a medium-sized dog. Until recently she's been in really good health, apart from some stiffness in her back legs due to mild arthritis, but last week she suddenly went downhill and was brought into the surgery by her owner, the equally aged Mrs Pearson.

'I'm really worried about Peppy,' said Mrs Pearson as she encouraged an obviously miserable and reluctant Peppy into the consulting room, 'she's not been right for a couple of days now and what with her age and everything, I'm really concerned about her.'

It took a little while and some detective work to get to the diagnosis, but, by the end of the consultation, it seemed likely that Peppy was suffering from a problem that is increasingly common in older female dogs – a womb infection. This occurs when the lining of the womb becomes thickened and infected, and leads to a range of symptoms, including lethargy and depression, as Peppy demonstrated, plus excessive thirst and usually a mucky discharge from the back end. In Peppy's case, however, there was no mucky discharge and it required an ultrasound scan after the consultation to confirm the diagnosis.

Once I knew what the problem was, there was no time to waste as a closed womb infection like this, where there is no leakage from the back end, is potentially very dangerous and even life-threatening. We stabilized Peppy on some intravenous fluids before taking her through to the operating theatre for surgery to remove her womb. These operations are much more serious than a routine neutering operation, due to the age and frail state of the patients, but Peppy pulled through fine and, as I write this, she's just been back in for her 3 day check-up and is almost back to her old self, much to the immense relief of Mrs Pearson!

Cases like this show that while we do face plenty of challenges looking after our aging pet population, modern veterinary care can often hold back the effects of time and keep our pets fit and healthy for many years – and who knows, by the time I retire, perhaps I'll be seeing thirty year old cats and dogs in the surgery!

THE STRANGE CASE OF THE SWOLLEN FACE

During the Christmas period, there are some cases that are much more common than at other times of the year – turkey bones stuck in the throat, Christmas pud related indigestion and so on (although if you took notice of last week's column and cooked up a healthy Christmas dinner for your pet, hopefully vets around the country won't be seeing so many of these kind of problems this year!) There are, however, some conditions that are much less common over the festive season, and in the run up to Christmas this year I saw a case that I would normally expect to see in mid-summer, not mid-winter.

It involved Digger the Jack Russell and, as you'll see, his name was a clue to the cause of his problems.

'His face is all swollen up,' announced Digger's owner, a gruff farmer from one of the more remote Cotswold villages, 'he was fine last night, then this came up this morning, after he'd been out in the fields.'

It wasn't hard to spot the problem – Digger's face was completely puffed up down one side, with his lip ballooning out and his eye half closed.

'If this was summer, I'd say he's been stung by a bee or bitten by a snake,' I said as I examined Digger on the consulting table, 'but as it's the middle of winter, I'm a bit confused.'

'Well, he didn't get his name for nothing,' replied Digger's owner, 'he's a terrible digger, so maybe he's dug up a bee or something and it's stung him?'

I'd never heard of a bee sting in the depths of winter – all self-respecting bees should be fast asleep, hibernating until the spring – and as for snake bites, they're rare enough in the summer let alone the winter. Still, I couldn't think of any alternative ideas, so I set about examining his mouth more closely for the telltale black sting or pinprick hole that often indicates a bee sting, or the paired fang marks from an adder bite.

I really wasn't expecting to find anything, but after a couple of seconds, there it was – a tiny hole on the inside of his gum.

'I think you could be right,' I said, pointing out the hole, 'that's what we see when they've tried to eat a bee and have been stung in the mouth, so I think old Digger here's been living up to his name and digging up a poor sleepy bee.'

'That sounds about right,' nodded Digger's owner with a resigned look on his face, 'he's always been a good dog, but he's too nosey for his own good.'

A quick injection of a steroid anti-inflammatory was all that was required to get Digger's swollen face back down to normal – but given his character, I doubt very much whether he'll have learnt his lesson, and I wouldn't be at all surprised to see him back in the surgery again with another problem related to his nosey nature – I just hope he doesn't dig up anything more dangerous than a bee next time!

THE SPRINGER WHO LOST HIS SPRING

One of the most vital and yet most fragile systems in the body is the nervous system, and when it goes wrong or is damaged, the results can be catastrophic for the animal involved. Thankfully, animals have evolved many effective protective mechanisms to keep their precious neurological equipment safe, including a thick skull and layers of cushioning fluid around the brain. The most amazing protective structure is the spine though, as it not only protects the vital spinal cord, which carries all the nerve messages from the brain to the body, but it also does this while allowing animals to move and flex their bodies easily.

The spine is composed of many sections called vertebrae. These bones have holes in their centers through which the spinal cord passes, and smaller canals running out sideways, along which nerves run out to the muscles and organs of the body. The vertebrae are linked to each other via special discs of cartilage, which allow the bones to move and also cushion any stresses to the spine. These discs are vital components of the spinal column, but they can be the cause of serious problems if they are damaged.

In Basil the Springer spaniel, who I saw yesterday, for example, one of the discs in his spine was the cause of a very serious problem. He came in on Monday, because his owner had found him lying collapsed on the kitchen floor. He tried to get up when she approached him, but he couldn't manage to get his legs to lift him, and he collapsed back down again. His owner rushed him down to the surgery, where we examined him straightaway.

My first thought when I saw him was that he'd suffered a disc problem, as it is one of the most common causes of this kind of symptom in a middle-aged dog like Basil. Although it is most common in certain breeds of dog, such as dachshunds because of their unnaturally long backs, it can occur in any dog. The problem itself is very similar to a 'slipped disc' in people – one of the discs lying between two vertebrae moves or swells or breaks up, and then presses on the spinal cord, which runs just below it. The symptoms the animal suffers depends on how much pressure the damaged disc exerts on the spinal cord. A mild prolapsed disc (as the damaged disc is known) will just cause minor problems with coordination and some pain, whereas a severe case will cause total paralysis of the animal's legs, and can even cause incontinence and serious pain. In Basil's case, the damage was severe, he was unable to move his back legs at all, and he was obviously in some pain.

Our first move was to take an x-ray, and this confirmed the diagnosis, as we could see the narrowing of the spine associated with a slipped disc. With the diagnosis made, we gave Basil a large dose of an anti-inflammatory, which can help reduce the swelling in the spine, and some painkillers. Then we rang up a specialist orthopaedic vet to book him in for an emergency referral in the morning.

He went off the next morning, and I've just had confirmation from the specialists that he has indeed got a severe disc problem, and they are planning to operate on him this afternoon. With a bit of luck, he'll make a full recovery, but nothing is certain with a serious injury to the spine. Whatever happens, he'll have to take life a little more easily in the future, otherwise he'll be at risk of the problem returning.

Suggestions for Dog Names

Abby
Abel
Angus
Annie
Archie
Axle

Bailey
Blue
Brandy
Bruce
Buddy
Buster

Cassie
Charlie
Chelsea
Chip
Chloe
Cody

Daisy
Dixie
Duchess
Duke
Dusty
Dylan

Ebony
Echo
Edgar

Ellie
Elmer
Emerson

Fable
Felix
Fido
Floyd
Frisbee
Fritz

Gatsby
Genie
Goldie
Gunner
Gusto
Gypsy

Harley
Heidi
Holly
Homer
Honey
Hunter

Iggy
Inca
Indigo
Ipod
Iris
Ivy

Jack
Jade
Jasmine
Jasper
Jilly
Joker

Kaiser
Katie
Kermit
Kiki
Kipling
Kosmo

Lady
Laser
Liberty
Limbo
Lucky
Lulu

Maggie
Maverick
Max
Missie
Molly
Murphy

Nacho
Nellie
Newton

Ninja
Nudge
Nutmeg

Ollie
Orbit
Orion
Oscar
Otis
Ozzie

Paisley
Patsy
Petra
Phoenix
Pickles
Princess

Quasi
Queenie
Quiche
Quicksilver
Quincy
Quirky

Rambo
Rebel
Rocky
Rolly
Roxanne
Rusty

Sadie
Sam
Sandy
Sasha
Scoobie
Sparky

Tango
Tasha
Texas
Toby
Trixie
Trouper

Ulysses
Uma
Urchin
Ursa
Ursula
Utopia

Velvet
Vince
Vinny
Violet
Vixen
Voodoo

Wanda
Wellington
Whiskey

Willow
Winston
Woody

Xanadu
Xanthus
Xavier
Xena
Xerox
Xray

Yabba
Yahoo
Yankee
Yogi
Yo-Yo
Yummy

Zelda
Zeus
Ziggy
Zipper
Zodiac
Zorro

Useful Websites

The following sites contain a variety of advice that is invaluable to dog owners. Please note, their inclusion here is in no way an endorsement of these sites. Any medical advice on these sites is no substitute for going to your vet.

www.canine-epilepsy-guardian-angels.com
Packed full of advice for owners of epileptic dogs and vets, this site also provides advice on other canine illnesses.

www.dogbreedersgallery.co.za
Aimed at dog owners in South Africa, this site has advice on a number of doggy topics, including feeding a raw meat diet and advice on picking the best dog for you.

www.dogchannel.com
As well as covering a variety of topics, like living with a dog, puppy care, dog activities and adopting a dog in the USA, this site has an excellent section on the different illnesses and ailments dogs can suffer.

Go to the home page and click on "MEDICAL CONDITIONS," and you'll be brought to an A-Z of ailments.

www.dogfriendly.com
This American site features over 1000 dog friendly locations throughout the USA and Canada, as well as world-wide travel guides.

www.dogster.com
A US site crammed full of doggy information covering everything the dog owner needs to know.

www.dogsincanada.com
A site devoted to "dogs and their Canadians," there's a number of helpful dog care articles on their site. This is the companion to the magazine of the same name.

To find articles, click on "articles" on the home page on the menu below the "Dogs in Canada" logo.

www.dogstrust.co.uk
The UK's no.1 dog charity site's main aim is to get people to adopt one of their dogs or to sponsor one, but they also have a good selection of fact sheets on everyday dog problems. To find it go to 'Dog A-Z' on the home page, then, on the left hand side, click on 'FACTSHEETS AND DOWNLOADS.'

www.lostdogsuk.com
If you lose your dog in the UK, you can list them on this site for free.

www.war-dogs.com
War Dogs is a site aimed at "America's forgotten heroes," the dogs who have saved soldiers and civilians' lives.

www.whosyadoggy.com
The site exists to help reunite lost dogs with their owners in America, Canada, Australia and New Zealand. You can post free lost and found dog ads.

NOTE: If your dog goes missing and he or she has been microchipped, always contact your microchipping company first.

Index